D0909107

Verse with Prose
from Petronius to Dante

Carl Newell Jackson Lectures

Verse with Prose From Petronius to Dante

THE ART AND SCOPE OF THE MIXED FORM

Peter Dronke

Harvard University Press
Cambridge, Massachusetts
London, England
1994

Library of Congress Cataloging-in-Publication Data

Dronke, Peter.
Verse with prose from Petronius to Dante : the art and scope of
the mixed form / Peter Dronke.
p.   cm.
"Carl Newell Jackson lectures [1992]"—Half-t.p.
Includes bibliographical references and index.
ISBN 0-674-93475-X
1. Classical literature—History and criticism.   2. Literature,
Medieval—Classical influences.   3. Literary form.   I. Title.
PA3014.L49D76   1994
880'.09—dc20
93-4282
CIP

Contents

Preface

In April 1992 I had the honour of delivering the Carl Newell Jackson Lectures at Harvard University. This book is essentially a record of the four lectures as they were given, though a number of revisions have been made and notes and references added. There is a special reason in this instance for not introducing substantial additions or changes to the spoken version. As such, the subject—the mixed form, verse with prose, in the West from the first century A.D. to the thirteenth—is enormous. Yet it is also elusive: there were so many kinds of mixed form in the period, so many ways of combining verse with prose, so many uses, from the most poetic to the most prosaic, to which such combinations could be put. The advantage of broaching the topic in a brief series of lectures was that these—like the topic itself—could keep a certain elusiveness. It was possible to proceed evocatively rather than systematically. It was clear, in such a situation, that there could be no question of an exhaustive history or an all-encompassing theory. The problems of cultural continuities, of genre and definition, which lurk to ambush the historian and the theorist on their highway, present no dangers to a traveller who chooses to go by a smaller, unpaved route.

I have tried to exemplify "the art and scope of the mixed form" by singling out a range of instances for consideration, and by critical interpretation of certain key passages in my chosen texts. The route I decided to follow came to reveal quite a few discoveries and surprises. Some of the most individual texts at which I paused were little known, some had never been brought into a discussion of mixed forms before. Yet I believe that each of the very diverse texts selected for more detailed consideration is in its way outstanding. I hope that, by grouping these texts together and focussing on their intellectual and imaginative processes, a picture may begin to emerge that is more engrossing than discrete critical readings on their own would be. The picture, to be sure, is an impressionist's first sketch, of a landscape in which much remains unfamiliar and barely defined. It will be for others to capture other aspects of that landscape, to depict it with the help of more elaborate techniques, or indeed to start an excavation on the site, following the lure of rich archaeological finds.

This book is intended for all who have been drawn to any aspect of ancient or medieval literature, whether as general readers or as specialists. With non-specialist, and also comparative, readers in mind, I have offered English translations—literal but I hope not arid—of all passages cited from Greek, Latin, and the diverse medieval vernaculars. While the notes supply the most necessary documentation for specialists, I have resisted the temptation to expand this documentary material, or to dwell to any extent on scholarly controversies. Bibliographical references have deliberately been kept down to a scale commensurate with that of the lectures themselves. Several of the texts that enter my discussion—such as Boethius' *Consolatio Philosophiae* or Dante's *Vita Nuova*—have a huge, ever more abundant, literature devoted to them; others, such as Marguerite Porete's *Mirouer des simples ames,* still have very little. To have adduced Boethian or Dantesque scholarship in all its fullness here would have been quite out of proportion. My principle for the most-discussed and the least-discussed writers has been the same: to cite as far as possible authoritative and recent editions, and (where available) commentaries, but to limit references to secondary literature to what is essential in relation to my argument.

If we can see the use of mixed forms as a constant in western literature (to speak of their oriental counterparts lies outside my competence), the paradox remains that they are among the most vital of European forms and among the most evanescent. At times, while perceiving the vitality, we can also see that the evanescence is, as it were, inbuilt. Thus for instance in October 1992, the month in which I completed these lectures for publication, there appeared in

Italian bookshops Pier Paolo Pasolini's posthumous work *Petrolio,* his immense—unfinished, and at the same time intrinsically fragmentary—homage to Petronius. To cite in translation some of Pasolini's solemnly teasing introductory phrases:

> The whole of PETROLIO (from the second draft onwards) will have to be presented in the form of a critical edition of an unpublished text (considered as a monumental work, a modern *Satyricon*). Of such a text there survive four or five manuscripts, concordant and discordant, of which some contain facts and others not, etc. Thus the reconstruction takes advantage of the collation of the various manuscripts extant (among which, for example, are two apocrypha, with curious variants . . .), . . . but also of the contribution of other materials: letters by the author (about whose identity there is a still unresolved philological problem, etc.), letters by friends of the author who know about the manuscript (disagreeing with one another), oral testimonies reported in journals or miscellanies, popular songs, etc.[1]

What Pasolini projected was thus an exuberant *discordia concors*—Menippean, prosimetric, shape-shifting, analysing itself and undermining itself. He saw that such a choice could still in our time offer a writer enthralling polysemous openings. The ancient and medieval writers who worked with mixed forms displayed their own varieties of *discordia concors*; some of these will be discussed and I hope illuminated in the course of this little book.

When I arrived in Cambridge, Massachusetts, last April, I was full of apprehension: the giving of the Jackson Lectures loomed as a daunting ordeal. A week later, as I was returning to my own Cambridge, apprehension had changed into exhilaration. This was due to the marvellous welcome and kindness shown by old friends—Margaret Alexiou, Charles Segal, Jan Ziolkowski—as well as by new—in particular Gregory Nagy and Holly Davidson. It was also due to having had a quite unusually responsive and generous audience, and to the delight of many hours of stimulating informal discussion, in which I learnt much from colleagues in a wide range of fields.

My special thanks, finally, to Gregory Nagy, Peter Rickard, and Patrick Sims-Williams, for patiently and expertly answering questions on points of Sanskrit, Old French, and Old Irish, and to the friends who have read the complete typescript and given me their valuable comments: Michael Reeve (who first drew my attention to the Greek prosimetric papyrus finds), Jill Mann, Marina Warner, and—perhaps more than ever—Ursula Dronke.

P.D.
Cambridge
February 1993

VERSE WITH PROSE
FROM PETRONIUS TO DANTE

I

Menippean Elements

Any allusion to the mixed form—verse with prose—if it is made in the context of European literature, tends to conjure up, first and foremost, Menippean satire. This initial association is indeed not wrong—yet it could also be too limiting: the uses of the mixed form, in many periods, extend far beyond the Menippean. Menippus himself, writing in the third century B.C., is known to have alternated prose and verse in his compositions. But as these are lost save for some titles and a handful of quotations, how far his verse consisted of fresh composing, rather than of citing or parodying others, remains a moot point. Frequent shifts between prose and verse can be found likewise in certain archaic works of a rather different character, such as Pseudo-Herodotus' *Life of Homer* or the anonymous *Contest between Homer and Hesiod*[1]—works that probably in their earliest formation go back to a period well before Menippus himself. And what is deemed to be Menippean in later centuries is usually defined in terms of content, technique and tone, rather than by the presence of verse in the midst of prose.

The alternation of verse with prose can be an intrinsic aspect of how a work is organised, or an incidental one. It seems to be incidental—for the most part—in the writings of Lucian, the most prolific extant Menippean of the ancient world. Many of Lucian's dialogues contain little or no verse, and what there is tends to be quoted, or adapted, to various comic ends; it is only occasionally—as in *Zeus Tragoidos*—freely invented. Amid the immense number and range of works that use both verse and prose in ancient and medieval Europe, I shall look chiefly at ones whose verse is more than quotation or parody, incidental adornment or allusion—ones where the verse is substance rather than accident, where verse and prose have become consubstantial.

For a medievalist, there is a certain historical precedent for such a distinction and choice of limits. In the Latin Middle Ages, the mixed form came to be known as *prosimetrum*. The earliest instance of the term that I have found occurs in a treatise on the art of composition, *Rationes dictandi,* by Hugh of Bologna, ca. 1119.[2] Hugh first demarcates prose composition and "metrical, that is measured, composition" *(metricum . . . id est mensuratum dictamen)*. He then distinguishes three branches of the measured: *carmina* (quantitative verse), *rithmi* (where what counts is the number of syllables and how the sounds harmonise), and thirdly "the mixed form *(mixtum),* which is called *prosimetrum*". Hugh, that is, defines the *prosimetrum* as a branch of poetic composition. For him the poetic aspect is integral to the form and determines its nature, even if "we call it a *prosimetrum* when a part is expressed in verse and a part in prose".

Yet if, encouraged by this hint from Hugh of Bologna, we set aside the works in which "the poetry does not matter", this still leaves an enormous field. To delimit further, I shall try to focus on works where the conjunction of verse and prose shows unusual or imaginative features, and shall consider more closely some of the ways in which the two modes came to be interrelated and combined. In medieval Latin in particular, verse could occur in, and indeed become intrinsic to, such diverse contexts—chronicles and saints' lives, consolations and love-letters, mythography and mirrors for princes—that any attempt to chart the uses of the mixed form comprehensively might lead to mere enumeration and summary description, rather than to a critical enquiry and an enquiry into poetics.[3]

So in these investigations I shall highlight only a few ancient and medieval works, or rather, highlight a few moments in those works that seem to me to illustrate creative ways of deploying the mixed form. In the present chapter I shall touch briefly on five ancient and three medieval texts that show Menippean elements. In the second I shall suggest some of the diverse possibilities of allegory in relation to the mixed form. There I shall begin with two works filled with allegorical beings, works that are strikingly different from one another—Methodius' *Symposium,* and Martianus Capella's *Marriage of Philology and Mercury.* I think that each of these two, in its own way, can illuminate aspects of the subtlest and most moving *prosimetrum* of the ancient world, Boethius' *Consolation of Philosophy.* I shall pause longer with this work, adding one or two illustrations of how, in the Middle Ages, Boethius' achievement was creatively renewed. Neither in the discussion of allegory nor in the topics of the third and fourth chapters shall we altogether lose sight of Menippean elements: some of these, it will emerge, recur as constants in European literature, and lurk in contexts where we might least expect them.

The theme of the third chapter will be narrative and the mixed form. Here, to adumbrate the poetic and imaginative potential, it will be vital to risk some comparative suggestions—even from areas where I can claim no specialist knowledge but must rely on expert help from friends. I shall choose examples from two kinds of narrative. One that—like Icelandic scholars—I shall call "poets' sagas": beginning with the Herodotean *Life of Homer* and the *Contest between Homer and Hesiod,* but comparing and contrasting the uses of the mixed form in these works with its uses in medieval vernacular poets' sagas, in Irish, Norse, and Provençal. The second, complementary topic is the rôle of verse in certain kinds of romantic adventures. Here I shall touch on aspects of two ancient texts—the romances of Alexander and Apollonius—suggesting, especially for the second, how it may illuminate a medieval text and be illuminated by it.

In the final chapter, I want to illustrate and analyse some of the most personal uses of the mixed form. While a number of prosimetrical texts, Menippean, allegorical, and narrative, make use of the first person singular, there are also certain exceptional, intensely individual texts where this becomes something more, where the writer creates, to adapt Leo Spitzer's phrase, both "a poetic and an empirical 'I'".[4] One could speak of autobiographical writings in the mixed form—yet Spitzer's expression has the advantage of stressing that here too we have to do with literary constructs, with artefacts and not outpourings, with writers who are well aware of the distinctions between the 'I' who writes, the "empirical 'I'" who is projected as protagonist, and the "poetic 'I'" who represents humanity. The culmination of these unusual uses of the mixed form does not occur till the thirteenth century, and it is in the vernacular, not the classical, languages—with Marguerite Porete in France, Mechthild of Magdeburg in Germany, and Dante in Italy.

Scholars often characterise Menippean satire without specific reference to form. That Menippeans tend to alternate prose with verse is not forgotten, yet this is not regarded as an essential feature of the tradition. Two of the most stimulating critics who have taken this approach, Northrop Frye and Mikhail Bakhtin, have had Renaissance and modern authors, rather than ancient ones, especially in mind. To cite Frye: "no one will challenge the statement that the literary ancestry of *Gulliver's Travels* and *Candide* runs through Rabelais and Erasmus to Lucian".[5] Frye is concerned to distinguish Menippean satire from the novel: it "differs from the novel in its characterisation, which is stylised rather than naturalistic, and presents people as mouthpieces of the ideas they represent".[6] Where the novelist's concern is more with human and social relationships, "the Menippean satirist, dealing with intellectual themes and attitudes, shows his exuberance in intellectual ways, by piling up an enormous mass of erudition about his theme, or in overwhelming his pedantic targets with an avalanche of their own jargon".[7] While Frye does not discuss the contribution of the verses to Menippean writings, he perceptively mentions certain more recent *prosimetra*—such as those of Thomas Love Peacock and Lewis Carroll—among his examples of Menippea.

Bakhtin first felt the need to sketch and define the Menippean tradition in 1929, in order to illuminate two late stories by Dostoevsky: *Bobok* and *The Dream of a Ridiculous Man*.[8] I shall allude to only a few of Bakhtin's fertile observations, that are of special interest for the texts on which I'll focus. Bakhtin sees in Menippean satire, along with other genres such as the mime, an imaginative freedom that deliberately rejects decorum and unity, that blends the serious and the comic, the high and the low. Like the early Platonic dialogues,

Menippean satires show truth not as ready-to-hand or imposed, but as emerging dialogically, among people who search for it together. Often such satires include fantastic elements—journeys to heaven or the underworld, or into unbelievable lands on earth, or again the work may begin with a dream, or the discovery of a wondrous manuscript or letter, and

> the fantastic serves here not in the positive embodiment of the truth, but in the search after the truth, its provocation and, most importantly, its testing . . . The menippea is a genre of "ultimate questions". In it ultimate philosophical positions are put to the test.[9]

It is a genre replete with contrasts and paradoxes: the wise man who is truly free even when he is a slave, the violent alternations of fortune, luxury and poverty, human rises and falls. There is a sense that all the extremes of human destiny are simply so many rôles played out on the stage of the world; but there are also evocations of different worlds, of utopias.

The one thing that neither Frye nor Bakhtin discussed directly is the Menippean linguistic and stylistic range. I believe this can be seen to mirror and enhance the features they alluded to. In style and diction, too, the Menippean elements tend to a willed lack of unity and decorum, or better, to a *discors concordia*. Varro's fragments include coinages and recherché words, alongside slang and rude words, and many Greek words and phrases; Petronius moves easily from the depiction of loud coarseness to the gentlest lyricism. In works that have something Menippean about them, the language, like the tone and attitude and subject-matter, has its oscillations: the high style and the low, the macaronic use of native and foreign expressions, the interspersing of exotic words among familiar ones, the transitions from exalted prayers to earthy jests—all these aspects of language qualify each other, relativise each other, at times we could say undermine each other. The alternation of verse and prose can likewise contribute vividly to such a *discors concordia*. Perhaps more than Frye or Bakhtin I would wish to stress the concepts of relativising and undermining. Truth emerges through testing—but this testing often takes the form of undermining the sureness of authorities, institutions and points of view, just as, linguistically, of undermining an established decorum of genres and diction. The distinctions between the well-demarcated regions of the cosmos—heaven, earth, hell, the familiar and unfamiliar parts of the globe—may also be undermined. So, too, some of the texts that feature allegories deliberately mix beings of different kinds of reality, or deliberately question received dichotomies, such as matter and spirit, body and soul.

I should now like to turn to passages in particular texts in order to illustrate some of these points. For the earliest testimonies this is peculiarly difficult. From a visit to the museum in Paestum, thirty years ago, I remember a metope of the sixth century B.C. that bore the legend: "Heracles slaying the Nemean lion". It showed about half the heel of one large male foot, nothing more: everything else had been sketched in by a scholar of the twentieth century A.D. The situation for the oldest Menippean texts—Menippus himself in Greek, Varro in Latin—seems to me remarkably similar.

We know wretchedly little about Menippus: we can say that he was born around 300 B.C., a Phoenician and perhaps a slave,[10] that he belonged to the Cynic school of thought, that in his writings he mixed prose with verse—and hardly more. Nonetheless, even the few sentences that survive from his piece, "Diogenes up for Sale", indicate some distinctive aspects of his satire:

φησὶ δὲ Μένιππος ἐν τῇ Διογένους Πράσει ὡς ἁλοὺς καὶ πωλούμενος ἠρωτήθη τί οἶδε ποιεῖν. ἀπεκρίνατο, "ἀνδρῶν ἄρχειν". καὶ πρὸς τὸν κήρυκα, "κήρυσσε," ἔφη, "εἴ τις ἐθέλει δεσπότην αὐτῷ πρίασθαι."...
θαυμάζειν τ᾽ ἔφη εἰ χύτραν μὲν καὶ λοπάδα ὠνούμενοι κομποῦμεν· ἄνθρωπον δὲ μόνῃ τῇ ὄψει ἀρκεῖσθαι. ἔλεγε τῷ Ξενιάδῃ τῷ πριαμένῳ αὐτόν, δεῖν πείθεσθαι αὐτῷ, εἰ καὶ δοῦλος εἴη· καὶ γὰρ ἰατρὸς ἢ κυβερνήτης εἰ δοῦλος εἴη, πεισθῆναι ἂν αὐτῷ.[11]

When Diogenes was taken prisoner and put up for sale, he was asked what he could do. He answered: "Govern men". And to the auctioneer he said: "Proclaim it, in case someone wants to buy a master for himself"...

And he said he was amazed that, before we buy a pot or dish, we try whether it rings true, but a man we are satisfied just to look at. To Xeniades, who bought him, he said: "You must obey me, even if I am a slave: for if a doctor or a helmsman were a slave, people would obey him".

The sardonic, irreverent tone and the paradoxes of the world upside down serve the testing of truth. Who is really a master, who really a slave? There is an element of utopia here, evoking a different kind of world, where inner integrity and a keen intellect, and not the accident of birth, would determine who governs. There are certain contexts—curing a patient, or steering a ship unerringly—where the world's "normal" distinctions—master/slave, high/low—are ignored, or suspended as long as is needed for a safe treatment or a safe journey. For that space of time there is a levelling, or even—as in the medieval Feast of Fools—a reversal, of everyday rôles. Here at least it seems difficult to doubt Bakhtin's claim that Menippean satire has popular roots, that it is animated by the spirit of carnival.

The examples from Rome, on the other hand, show Menippean satire being used by men who, unlike Menippus, are themselves high-born and wealthy. Yet they too can assume Saturnalian licence, and imagine—for a brief time—a world that's levelled or a world upside down.

In the case of the erudite, prolific Varro (116–27 B.C.), we have nearly six hundred small fragments extant; but as they stem from almost a hundred distinct Menippean satires, of which not even one is well enough documented to allow us to reconstruct its scenario with confidence, the problems are again as with the heel on the Paestum metope. We know from Varro's friend Cicero that he composed his own verses for his Menippea, in a variety of metres;[12] polymetry is indeed a characteristic of later ancient and medieval examples. Traces of this variety can still be glimpsed in Varro's fragments. So too the titles that survive, often in Greek or else bilingual, indicate some of Varro's targets: he mocks excesses in food, drink and sex, and mocks the heroism men associate with wars; he mocks superstition in religion and charlatanry in philosophy; he is fascinated by the nature of madness and of what the world calls mad.

He uses coinages to make sexual satire pungent: at the luxurious resort of Baiae, he claims

> quod non solum innubae fiunt communis, sed etiam veteres repueras-cunt et multi pueri puellascunt—[13]

> that not only do unmarried girls become shared, but even old men begin to boy again, and many boys begin to girl.

In his scorning shafts directed against vinolence, Varro enjoys using the rude diminutives, *matella* and *matula,* for "chamberpot". The wine in the amphorae of the rich ends up in the common *matella* (102), and the title of one satire—*Est modus matulae: Περὶ μέθης* ("There's a limit to what a chamberpot can hold: On drunkenness")[14]—seems to imply that no guest should drink so much that, when he pisses into the communal *matula,* he leaves no space for the contributions of others. A fragment from this dialogue extends Varro's amused disdain even to Olympus (113):

> non vides ipsos deos, si quando volunt gustare vinum, derepere ad hominum fana et temetum ipsi illi Libero simpuio ministrari?

> Don't you see that the gods themselves, if they want to taste wine, slink into human sanctuaries, and even great Bacchus is served with the libational soupspoon?

Of particular interest to me as a medievalist is the group of twenty-six fragments from a satire entitled *Bimarcus.*[15] The name, according to the recent editor, Jean-Pierre Cèbe, means "the double Marcus", and alludes to the two-sided nature of Marcus Varro him-self. The fragments suggest this was a dialogue between his two "selves": one the persona of a consummate rhetorician, the other of an aspirant to a worthier, more serious ideal of philosophy—a kind of dialogue that foreshadows later ones in the European tradition. Thus Augustine's *Soliloquia* are dialogues between Augustinus and Ratio—"whether I myself or another, whether outside me or within me, I do not know: for it is this that I am trying hard to get to know".[16] Some medieval thinkers, such as Peter Abelard and Jean de Meun, likewise interpreted Boethius' arguments with Philosophia as

a dialogue between the author and his own reason.[17] In the eleventh
century, the poet-humanist Hildebert composes a *prosimetrum* of
dream dialogues between himself and a tall, radiant and beautiful
womanly being, whom we might take to be the Philosophia of
Boethius, but who turns out to be Hildebert's inner self.[18] In the
early twelfth century Petrus Alfonsi, a converted Jew, composes an
internal debate between Petrus and Moses—his new and his old
self,[19] and Peter Abelard a *Soliloquium* between Abaelardus and
Petrus.[20] The culmination of the genre is Petrarch's *Secretum,* the
many-faceted dispute between his two projections, Franciscus and
Augustinus.[21] In all these works a caustic Menippean note can at
times be heard; in all of them it implies, in Bakhtin's words about the
Menippean spirit, a "search after the truth, its provocation and . . . its
testing".

In Petronius' *Satyricon,* the testing of truth has far wider ram-
ifications. The differences between what the characters seem and
what they are, between their speeches and their actions, their
rhetoric and their nature, are crucial to nearly everything in the por-
tions of the work that have survived. The intriguing question that
has arisen concretely only in the last two decades is, whether Petronius was the first to make a certain creative leap, taking *prosimetrum*
and Menippean satire in the direction of a novel. Previously, any
suggestion that he might have had Greek predecessors for his exper-
iment was pure unfounded speculation. Now the publication of fifty
lines of the *Iolaus* fragment makes the problem more compelling. We
do not know if *Iolaus* is older than the *Satyricon,*[22] or was the first
Greek composition of its kind; if one can say with high probability
that the complete *Satyricon* was immense, there seems to be no way
of gauging the size of *Iolaus,* which might have been as brief as a
novella, and not at all of Petronian dimensions. Yet, as Peter Parsons
showed in his learned, fascinating reconstruction and discussion of
the *Iolaus* fragment, in some essential respects Petronius no longer
stands quite alone.[23]

In *Iolaus,* the unnamed protagonist learns secrets (ἀπόρρητα) from
a fellow-initiate (συμμύστης), who is a *gallus*—that is, one of the
lower-class, itinerant eunuch priests of Cybele. He learns to wear
women's clothes. Next he speaks twenty lines of verse in the
Sotadean metre (which is used in ribald as well as holy contexts),

addressing Iolaus and silencing a male prostitute (κίναιδος) who is also present. He claims to be a mystic (μυστικός) and to have mystic knowledge. The allusions in what the mystic then says he knows are very fragmentary, yet they seem to refer to matters of a different, not obviously religious, kind: intercourse, an oath, an unburied dead person,[24] a bastard child, lamentations of the father and the women in the house, a birthday-party where the prostitute acts as jester and Iolaus is about to have illicit sex (βεινεῖν). After the verses, which—unlike the poetic passages in Petronius—continue the narrative and advance the plot, the prose tells that Iolaus is being taught by the mystic, who has become a perfect (τέλειος) *gallus*[25] with the help of a trusted friend called Nicôn.

As Parsons pointed out, Petronius, like the Greek author, includes a brief appearance of a *cinaedus* (23)—a catamite who solicits custom by singing some Sotadean verses. I would add that, again apparently like the author of *Iolaus,* Petronius evokes sex in terms of lustful escapades, and at times with deliberately unrefined language (compare his use of *debattuere* [69, 3]—"to pound"—with βεινεῖν in *Iolaus*).[26] Petronius, moreover, depicts quite a few characters who are grotesque and emarginated—as the jesting *gallus* and the *cinaedus* seem to be in *Iolaus.* Again, as the Greek text allows the suspicion that the "mystic knowledge" revealed to Iolaus isn't nearly as holy as the initiate pretends, so more palpably in Petronius the mystic rites, in which first an anonymous enchantress (131) and then the priestess Oenothea (134–138) try to restore Encolpius' potency, reveal themselves as shabby hocus-pocus.

What we can observe at times in Petronius, though not in the brief extant portion of *Iolaus,* is a disturbing way of testing truth, which I would see as profoundly Menippean, and which is here intimately linked with the alternation of prose and verse. In Petronius this formal alternation can I believe become symbolic of an alternation of points of view—in the prose, that of the tragicomic narrative realm, with all its crudities and cruelties; in the poetry, that of the realm of an intense imagination.

Thus the bravura piece on the Civil War (119–124), much the longest poetic passage in the work, is attributed to Eumolpus, who in the prose narrative reveals himself a *louche,* cynical pederast and trickster, ludicrously pleased with his own verses, even though, when he recites them, he gets abused or in one case stoned. Yet when the narrator, Encolpius, first catches sight of him, Eumolpus' face "seemed to have an indefinable promise of greatness" (*videretur nescio quid magnum promittere,* 83); and Eumolpus' blazing poetic indictment of the horrors of war, even if at times it verges on bombast, can still move us in a way that no merely virtuoso composition could. It has the qualities—impassioned, resplendent, *and* histrionic—of the Trojan speech of the First Player in *Hamlet.* It undermines our previous perception of Eumolpus, to make us marvel, is this rascal capable of such inner grandeur? At the same time, the narrative perspective on Eumolpus is not wholly forgotten; thus we can be both moved and a little uneasy—as Hamlet was uneasy about the Player's Trojan declamation:

> Is it not monstrous that this Player heere,
> But in a Fixion, in a dreame of Passion,
> Could force his soule so to his own conceit . . .

Similarly, in the opening of the Circe episode (126–128), if we were to confine a summary of what happens to the prose narrative, it would be little more than this: The beautiful lady Circe, full of lascivious desire for low-born young men, sends her slave-girl Chrysis to Encolpius, to invite him to a rendezvous. He is overwhelmed by Circe's beauty, and heady with romantic longing for her, but, after blissful amorous foreplay, he finds, to his utter despair, that he is impotent, since, before meeting Circe, he had worn himself out coupling with the boy Giton.

The verses not only modify the external narrative, they are used, we might say, in polyphony. The prose alone would here make the protagonists caricatures—almost farcical, or, if one tried to empathise with them, embarrassing. Yet the three brief poetic moments in the episode evoke a totally different inner dimension. In the midst of the bathos of seduction, and love-play leading to impotence—humiliating Circe and Encolpius alike—Petronius reminds us again and again what heroic love and idyllic love can be. In the verses, which are written in couplets and hexameters, but have the movement of incantations, Jupiter is summoned to marvel at the beauty of Circe: "Here is the true Danae!" *(Haec vera est Danae!);* his divinity still hedges the flowers on the grass where Encolpius and Circe lay, where "the light, more brightly gleaming, graced our secret love" *(candidiorque dies secreto favit amori);* the failed Encolpius is like one whose illusory dream of gold in the night mocks his mind, that "twists and turns, engrossed, in the image of what's past" *(animus . . . in praeterita se totus imagine versat).* The total story here is simultaneously the demeaning happenings and half-theatricalised emotions in the prose, and the fleeting thoughts and images of erotic perfection in the poetry. It lies in the way these discordant elements act upon each other.

Unlike the texts mentioned so far, Seneca's brief Menippean satire has come down to us nearly complete (the only lacuna represents probably just one missing leaf in the archetype).[27] The earliest extant manuscripts (late ninth to tenth century) call Seneca's work *Divi Claudii apotheosis per saturam* (that is, "the apotheosis of the divine Claudius in a mixture of prose and verse"),[28] or *Ludus de morte Claudii* ("the play about Claudius' death"). In the period of these manuscripts we have some precious evidence for the connotations of *ludus, ludere* and related terms. In the year 876 Iohannes Immonides arranged for the presentation of his comic poetic masquerade, the *Cena Cypriani,* on two occasions: in the presence of the Pope, John VIII, at the Cornomannia, the Roman "Feast of Fools" that was celebrated after Easter; and before the Emperor Charles the Bald, who, according to the author, "applauded it joyfully, along with his French poets and his drinking Gauls".[29] Immonides introduces himself in his Prologue as the compère of his own show, in which the mime-players burlesque a whole series of biblical motifs: he himself enters, he says, miming, singing and jesting *(saltantem, cantantem, iocantem),* and he proclaims: "I shall play a satire"—*Satiram ludam.*[30] In the Epilogue, Immonides adds: "It has been my joy to play; Pope John, welcome me for my playing"—*Ludere me libuit; ludentem, papa Iohannes, /accipe.*[31] Immonides' *ludus* was not a play in dialogue form but a verse narrative with accompanying mime. While it would be too adventurous to suggest that Seneca's *ludus* enjoyed a performance similar to that of the *Cena* at this time, the title *Ludus de morte Claudii* indicates that it was at least perceived as a piece with performance potential.

In 969 we have another allusion to *ludi* which is suggestive, by Liutprand of Cremona, whose major work, the chronicle *Antapodosis,* itself shows Menippean touches—not only in its witty Greek title (literally, "tit-for-tat"), but in occasional poetic passages of truly Senecan malice and verve amid the prose.[32] In a shorter, autobiographic work, Liutprand alludes to the plays *(ludi)* in which, in Byzantium, on July 20, "the frivolous Greeks celebrate Elijah's ascent to heaven".[33] These Greek *ludi* don't survive, but again the allusion helps to explain why Seneca's frivolous celebration of Claudius' ascent to heaven should have been called a *ludus.*

Seneca uses the characteristically Menippean motif of a fantastic voyage—first to heaven, then, returning via earth, to the underworld. Seneca's heaven and celestial assembly are comic, just as they are in medieval parodies of otherworld visions, as well as in medieval fabliaux. While these on the whole avoid the supernatural, if they *are* set in heaven or hell, then the otherworld is reduced to fabliau dimensions—it becomes as full of trickery and foolishness as anywhere on earth.

Claudius in the *Ludus* is at first presented with rude humour: his "famous last words" are a fart, accompanied by the cry "Oh dear, I think I've shit myself!" *(vae me, puto, concacavi me!).*[34] His speech defect and his limp are also mocked. It is in heaven, where Claudius applies to be received as a god, like Augustus and Tiberius, that the satire takes on a more menacing aspect. The decisive voice against this new apotheosis is that of Augustus himself, who reminds the Olympians of all the murders for which Claudius had been responsible (11, 4):

Hunc deum quis colet? quis credet? Dum tales deos facitis, nemo vos deos esse credet.

Who will worship *him* as a god? who will believe it? If you make gods like that, no one will believe that *you* are gods.

As Claudius is expelled from heaven, and Mercury drags him down to the underworld, he invisibly watches his own funeral on earth: "everyone was joyous, full of mirth: the Roman people were walking as if free" (*omnes laeti, hilares: populus Romanus ambulabat tamquam liber,* 12, 2). Claudius now hears the dirge *(nenia)* being sung for his death. This begins ostensibly solemnly—calling for lamentation, praising the Emperor for his fine judgement *(pulchre cordatus),* his unmatched valour, his fleetness of foot, his exploits in battle . . . That this is a litany of heavy ironies is suddenly shown openly, as the "mourners" bring into the dirge a Menippean discord, undermining all they had sung before: they continue:

> Deflete virum, quo non alius
> potuit citius discere causas,
> una tantum parte audita,
> saepe neutra.

> Mourn for the man whom none could rival
> in the speed of mastering legal cases—
> hearing one side of the question only,
> often hearing neither.

When Claudius reaches the lower depths and sees all his victims, and is at once tried for multiple murder, it is a fitting "tit-for-tat" that Aeacus, judge of the underworld, condemns Claudius exactly as Claudius had condemned others—*altera tantum parte audita,* "with only one side heard".

Where in Petronius the realms of prose and poetry could undermine each other, here, in Claudius' dirge, the poetry undermines itself: the semblance of a lament for him turns into an outright charge against him.

I should now like to evoke briefly three medieval Latin texts that show original uses of Menippean elements. In the earliest of these, the author (though probably not influenced by Seneca's satire) exuberantly takes up the satiric motif of impossible fantasy voyages. The work is usually known as the *Cosmographia* of Aethicus Ister.[35] Yet the text presents itself not as a work by Aethicus, but by St Jerome, no less. It is Jerome who here claims to be the redactor, paraphraser and translator of excerpts of Aethicus,[36] an incomparable first-century pagan sage, a Scythian from Istria, who wrote in Greek. All this of course is high-spirited fabrication: the work was perpetrated probably in the earlier eighth century.[37]

In 1923 W. M. Lindsay suggested that this *Cosmographia* was a *prosimetrum:*

> Aethicus Ister seems to break out every now and then into Hesperic verse to relieve the monotony of the *Cosmographia*. (I suspect the "Istrian" to have been an Irishman, for the interposition of verse-passages is quite in the manner of the Irish saga.)[38]

While Lindsay's conjecture that the author was Irish has been accepted by many, though not all, later scholars, his complementary, and startling, idea—that the work includes passages of "Hesperic verse"—has never been followed up, or challenged. It is not quite accurate as it stands. In vocabulary, while the *Cosmographia* has a number of clusters of exotic words and Graecisms, a direct link with the strange words in the texts known as *Hisperica Famina* is hard to perceive,[39] and the chief principle of the verses in the *Famina* is not precisely paralleled in "Aethicus". In the *Famina* the lines, though their number of syllables varies enormously, have a decisive caesura, and the word at the caesura is bound by assonance to the word at the close of the line.[40] In the *Cosmographia,* both the available editions present the entire text as prose, and yet a number of the passages where the persona "Jerome" cites the persona "Aethicus" in direct speech are highly poetic. These passages, unlike Hisperic verses, show pervasive, insistent rhythmic parallelism, and rhymes that consist not of simple Hisperic pairs of assonances but often of veritable cascades.

To begin with an example (I shall risk offering a translation, though I am not sure that I have fully grasped all the unfamiliar words and coinages or the headlong syntax): According to "Jerome", "Aethicus" had told of the Meopari—a race known from no other source—who go pirating each year from early June till the first of November. They do not fear rough seas, for they travel in submarines, equipped with diving-mirrors—or we could say driving-mirrors, for with their help the Meopari can steer under water straight at the ships they want to capture. Their deadly skill at ramming leads "Aethicus" to a passionate effusion:

O tu mare brumericum,
catago multorum hominum,
—aquilarum pennas assumunt—[41]
naufragium   gentium   ad extremum,
ultra magnitudinem piscium   et belluarum
ac hominum   hamum,
triumphatorium   hostium
cachinfatorum   naufragium,
aulonium   navium,
privata vehicula nauclerium,
subsecuta iam morte periculum,
lymphaque arena   assumitur
et carina magna   trituratur,
trieris singultum rigatur,
scapha dolose opprimitur:
ululant naves maris,
mure vorante decipulam . . .[42]

Oh you stormy ocean,
downfall of many men
(they take on eagles' wings)—
ultimate wrecker of peoples,
immense fish-hook, hook of monsters,
hook of humanity,
triumphant wrecker
of infamous foes,
of palace-like ships,
of those who own private vessels,
peril where death at once follows,
and sand and water penetrate
and a great keel is crushed,
a trireme drenched in the gurgling,
a boat overwhelmed by cunning:
the ships on the ocean howl
as the mouse swallows the trap . . .

The longest and grandest passage of this kind is the sage's *laudatio* of Greece; there alliteration is as marked as rhyme. If, as Lindsay and many of his successors have thought, the author of the *Cosmographia* was an Irishman, I think these virtuoso passages may well correspond to the examples of *retoiric* or *roscad* in early Irish vernacular texts, where there is no hard and fast boundary between verse and prose, but groups of short sentences or clauses are given a marked rhythmic and structural parallelism, enhanced by alliteration and the use of rare and difficult words.[43] Towards the end of the *Cosmographia*, "Jerome" says that "Aethicus" made an epitome of Pythagoras' sayings, *rethorico more styloque prosodico valde obscuro*—"in the manner of rhetoric and in a very obscure prosodic style",[44] and once he even credits "Aethicus" with having composed a Greek *prosimetrum*.[45]

I would see the *Cosmographia* as comic in a Menippean way throughout. To show this fully would demand a lengthy discussion; in the present context I can touch only briefly on a few of the salient Menippean features. One is the parade of bogus authorities. "Aethicus" for instance calls upon Hiarcas (the Brahman sage who was visited by Apollonius of Tyana).[46] Hiarcas sits on his golden throne at the seashore, while "Aethicus" refutes him, and refutes "the philosophers Cluontes and Agrippus, the Scythian astrologers, and Mantuanus, who had argued for many vain notions".[47] These sages are recorded nowhere else. Perhaps "Mantuanus" means the poet Vergil rather than an unknown philosopher; at all events soon afterwards "Jerome" supports the claims of "Aethicus" to have seen various animals that are not met elsewhere, by reference to Lucan. Lucan "in his manuscripts *(in codicibus suis)* mentioned *hyminiones* and *chylixae,* and the venomous *epipharoi,* which, though they are as small as foxes, kill lions and pards and dragons with a single stab".[48] Needless to say, these manuscripts of Lucan's are as imaginary as the animals themselves.

The attitude of "Jerome" to "Aethicus" is another frequent source of Menippean mischief: he praises "Aethicus" as virtually omniscient, as the wisest of all philosophers, though a pagan; and yet at times "Jerome" dares to hint at scepticism. The first hint comes here, when he adds: "Lucan, observing these animals, set out to say as much; but Aethicus writes of many animals of which we have never heard or read otherwise". And a little later: "We are not refuting him, yet we do wonder, for we have read some arguments of philosophers, but have never yet found anyone else who said such mighty things".

At times the parody is of travellers' tales: when "Aethicus", who has sailed everywhere, climbs a mountain on a South Sea island peopled by sirens and poisonous fabled beasts called *cidrosistae,* at the summit he becomes incandescent: "in the sun's brightness he has a force of such radiance that scarcely anyone could be seen."[49]

"Aethicus" makes a voyage from Ceylon (Taprobane) to the pillars of Hercules, beyond Cadiz: "there he stayed a year, disputing with the [otherwise unknown] philosophers Aurelius and Harpocrates, and they were unable to solve any of his riddles". His skill in riddling and solving riddles is praised in many parts of the work. From the pillars "Aethicus" gradually made his way, via Spain, to Ireland, "and he stayed there for some time; and, pondering their volumes, he called the Irish 'idiots'".[50] To convey this, "Jerome" uses two strange expressions as alternatives—*idiomochos vel idiotistas*—but his meaning is only too clear. According to one recent scholar, this passage betrays an anachronism: the author did not even realise that the Irish had no books in the first century A.D.,[51] the period of sages like Hiarcas, in which "Aethicus" is said to live. I would suggest that the author knew this perfectly well, and that the mockery here—the unique instance in the work where book-learning is pilloried as ignorance—is a tilt, perhaps only jestingly hostile, at his countrymen. It is this passage, far more than the alleged Hisperic affinities, that strongly inclines me to believe that the author was indeed Irish.

Another target of his satire is the more extravagant legends about Alexander. He playfully outdoes these, inventing many that have no close parallel in other Alexander fictions. He knows, for instance, of a tremendous battle between Alexander and the Albanians, in which one billion men (ten thousand times a hundred thousand) fell.[52] He also knows things about the Amazons which no one else does: that they nurse minotaurs and centaurs, feeding them at their breast, who then, filled with the milk of human kindness, defend the Amazons against any foe.[53] Here "Jerome", whose comments on his "source" increasingly come to resemble those of the commentator, Kinbote, in Nabokov's *Pale Fire*—says: We do not reject this, or pass it on for acceptance. Philosophers do at times get carried away, for love of glory. Once "Jerome" goes further still: "Aethicus" in Greece told various things about Hercules and Apollo "which it is unlawful for us to research or to accept".[54] But at the end all is well again: when "Aethicus" explains that rivers stem from the sea, and lose their saltiness as they flow further away from it, "Jerome" adds that "in this the Philosopher discoursed more beautifully than all the other sages we have investigated".[55] This concluding sentence is followed by an alphabet, of twenty-three elaborate, fantastic letters, which "Aethicus" invented; he named each letter in a word that is pure jabberwocky: Alamon, Becah, Cathu, Delfoy. . .

Older scholars such as Manitius shook their heads over the *Cosmographia:* they saw it as an ignorant but serious attempt at a work of learning, from the darkest of the dark ages.[56] More recently elements of parody and satire have been noted, yet still scholars have affirmed the presence of earnestly intended didactic elements as well. My own sense is of a work that is Menippean to the core. It has the tendency, well noted by Bakhtin and Frye as characteristic of the genre, of expanding into an encyclopaedic farrago—a tendency that reaches its culmination in Rabelais. The *Cosmographia* shows undiluted inventive delight in language, in fabrication, in pseudo-authorities, in the send-up of accepted wisdom about strange places, people and times. The opening pages, about God, the war in heaven, and the creation, deliberately lull the reader into a false sense of solemnity: as soon as the author turns to the sublunary world, exuberant impishness reigns.

A playfulness of a gentler and subtler, yet still essentially Menippean, kind pervades a very different work, of the late ninth century, which again is a *prosimetrum*. Notker the Stammerer, or Notker the Poet, who spent virtually his whole life in the cloister of Sankt Gallen, had in the 860s composed some forty lyrical sequences for feasts of the Church year—a cycle of poetic creations of incomparable concentration, delicacy and inwardness.[57] In the year 883 he was asked to write a life of his monastery's patron saint. The trouble was, there were no fewer than four lives of Gallus in existence already, including two by leading writers of the previous generation: a prose life by the humanistic scholar-poet Walahfrid Strabo, who had died in 849 in the nearby abbey of Reichenau, Sankt Gallen's keenest rival in culture; and another life, in hexameters, ca. 850, which may be by the exceptionally learned Ermenrich of Ell-wangen, who had been a monk at both monasteries. How was Notker to meet the challenge of surpassing his predecessors, of telling yet again a hagiographic tale that was already almost too well known, without creating something edifying but boring? Notker decided to use a form that had rarely been used for hagiography before: the *prosimetrum*.[58] It is a tragic loss that only fragments of this *Life of Gallus* survive; yet there is enough to perceive its originality and audacity. Here Notker shows an extrovert side to his writing which one would hardly have thought possible from his religious lyrics: it is a little as if George Herbert had also written *The Dunciad*. And Notker does not *tell* the life of Gallus, the early Irish hermit: rather, his *prosimetrum* is a series of ironic probings of the question, what would it be like to retell familiar stories about a saint? What do the topoi of hagiography really amount to? Many of them are paro-died, shrewdly though not maliciously, in what survives of this *Vita*. What is Menippean is not so much the parodies as such, nor even the questioning of the legends—it is the shape-shifting of the poet, his use of diverse strategies for the testing of truth.

The opening shows Notker inviting a young disciple of his, called Hartmann, to collaborate in composing Gallus' life, in a series of mock-heroic Sapphic stanzas. At first he addresses the boy in absurd hyperboles of praise:

> Ultima saecli generate meta
> Vincis antiquos lyrico poetas,
> Pindarum, Flaccum reliquosque centum,
>   Carmine maior . . .[59]

> You, begotten in this age's last extremity,
> surpass the lyric poets of antiquity—
> Pindar, Horace and a hundred others:
>   your song is greater . . .

Notker goes on to say his pupil rivals even the Old Testament prophets, David and Isaiah, in poetry: in other words, there is absolutely no excuse for him not to sing the deeds of Saint Gallus.

With the fourth strophe Notker suddenly becomes down-to-earth: Hartmann, he claims, is still too young, and hence too feeble, to compose anything unaided:

> Forsan et lassus titubas vel erras:
> Curro festinans, celerans levabo
> Et pedes firmans teneros praeibo
>   Calle modesto . . .

> Perhaps you're tired, tottering and erring:
> I shall at once run, buoying you up swiftly,
> steadying your tender feet I'll go before you
>   on this poor pathway . . .

He then, in a humorous, half-threatening fashion, asks his pupil to help:

> Sic ocellorum potiaris usu,
> Organo vocis careas nec umquam,
> Munus et gaudens manuum retentes:
>   Scribe quod hortor![60]

> So that you may enjoy the use of your dear eyes
> and never lack the organ of your voice
> and happily keep the function of your hands—
>   write what I bid you!

Hartmann replies in a different measure, the quatrains of Ambrosian hymns, protesting that he is quite unequal to the task. In his protest he alludes wittily to an ode of Horace's (II 5): he is as unready to bear the yoke of the poetic burden of Notker *(taurus fortissimus)* as the young girl imagined by Horace was to bear the yoke of love:

> Taurum cupis fortissimum
> Buclae tenellae iungere
> Vinumque mite disparis
> Gustu saporis tinguere.[61]

You long to yoke the mightiest bull
to a tender little heifer
and to spike a mellow wine
with a taste of different savour.

In the prose as well as the verse, the pupil is given a share in the dialogue. The way Notker arranges this confirms Bakhtin's insight into the Menippean tradition: truth is not presented as an "official version", it arises in the interplay of minds, in the mingling of earnest and game—and often in the mingling of verse with prose. The first prose passage begins with one of the longest sentences in the whole of Latin; it is constructed with extraordinary craft (in both senses of that word). Notker says in effect: I am far too little as a writer to depict all Gallus' hardships—"agitations, wanderings and turnings, ascents and descents, difficulties in the Alps, perils of seas, and new onslaughts of demons . . . crossing the ocean to exorcise the daughter of a duke . . . secretly clambering the rocks and precipices of the Alps to a hermitage that only goats can reach . . ." To do such exploits justice, we should need the brilliance of Walahfrid (that is, precisely of the writer whose *Vita* Notker had been commissioned to replace)—and I am too old to achieve that, and you too young. Notker evokes his old age (he was in fact forty-three!) in images that mimic Gallus' alleged heroic climbs—"my hands scarred by the teeth of rocks"—adding, "I who have grown a little toothless, a little blind, a little shaky *(edentulus, caeculus et tremulus),* partly through sickness, partly through senility".[62]

The whole passage belies itself. The lengthy alleged refusal to relate all that Walahfrid could relate so much better is in fact a new way of relating; Notker's syntax itself, as Berschin, the recent editor, well noted, here deliberately mirrors all the arduousness of Gallus' journeys, agitated and climbing the most difficult winding paths.[63] Another scholar, Vinay, rightly pointed out that from the earlier lives of Gallus, such as Walahfrid's, it is quite clear that the saint had to do none of the perilous things vouched for by Notker—either to reach his hermitage or to help the young duchess, Fridoburga—that the poet is here undermining the wonders of hagiography by parody.[64] After Notker's virtuoso sentences about all that he is *not* going to tell,

Hartmann the disciple replies: "You are going too far, Notker . . . so great a subject is indeed unsuited to our weak powers . . . you were inspired by divine grace when you decided it should be left to Walahfrid".[65]

My last illustration is from a text that was edited by Marvin Colker in 1975, under the title "Petronius redivivus".[66] It is a collection of fourteen distinct pieces, written probably in or near London in the late twelfth century. While a number of these are *exempla* which are concluded by verses, there is also one longer and more complex narrative where verses are interspersed amid the prose—where something of Petronius' form, as well as of his language and his misogynistic outlook, is reflected. An intimate firsthand knowledge of the *Satyricon* was rare at this time, though it can be documented among the polished men of letters who frequented the court of Henry II of England—John of Salisbury, Peter of Blois, Walter Map. It is I think quite possible that the author of "Petronius revived" was a member of this circle and found his first audience there. He used Petronius particularly to forge a striking language for erotic prose description and sardonic allusion to eroticism. The verses in the longer novella bring brief comments, as of a chorus, on the implications of the action, but are much less Petronian in style than the prose.

I am not wholly happy with Colker's characterisation of this novella, about the knight Zetus, his wife Hero, and her two Saracen lovers, as "a veritable chivalric romance".[67] I would sooner see it as a fabliau. Like his contemporary Walter Map in his story of Sadius and Galo[68] (which likewise features a girl called Hero, and which may be directly related), this author sets in a chivalric realm what is essentially an ignoble tale of tricking and countertricking, told with dark irony. Again like Map, he uses antique-sounding names for his personages—though the narrative plays in twelfth-century Spain. It is his way of distancing himself from the characters, and from some of the moral assumptions of a Christian world.

When the knight Zetus, who holds a Saracen chieftain, Antheus, prisoner in his tower, is away from home, his wife Hero unlocks the tower, gives herself to Antheus and helps him to escape. Zetus goes to the Saracen city, Murcia, in disguise, in pursuit of Hero, but when he has found her she deceives him yet again. She now takes a hideous renegade Christian as her lover, and tries to hand Zetus over to him, but fails. When Zetus and Hero return home, the knight does not, as friends and relatives advise, kill his faithless wife: instead he marries her off, humiliatingly, to his Saracen gardener. For Zetus is not excessively upset: as the author stresses throughout, what he really cared about was not his wife, but only his beautiful armour, which she had allowed the Saracens to steal. The novella is black comedy rather than romance.

What has not yet been remarked is that on at least two occasions this author wittily combines his echoes of Petronius with an echo of Boethius, from the *Consolation of Philosophy*. When Hero lusts for the imprisoned Antheus, the author comments in words that very closely follow those of Petronius' Chrysis about her mistress Circe (126):

> Nam quod servum te et humilem fateris, accendis desiderium aestu-antis. Quaedam enim feminae sordibus calent, nec libidinem conci-tant nisi aut servos viderint aut statores altius cinctos. Harena aliquas accendit aut perfusus pulvere mulio aut histrio scaenae ostentatione traductus . . . ego . . . numquam tamen nisi in equestribus sedeo.

> By admitting that you are a humble slave, you kindle her desire all the more. For some women are aroused only by what's low, their pas-sions don't stir unless they look at slaves, or errand-boys wearing their tunics too short. Others are set ablaze by combatants in the arena, or by a mule-driver smothered in dust, or by a vainglorious actor . . . As for me . . . in the theatre I never sit on any seats except those of knights.

The twelfth-century author, however, caps his Petronian enumer-ation of low-life lures—slaves, short-tunicked errand-boys, the arena, the dust-smothered mule-driver and the actor[69]—by a parody of a sentence from Boethius. When Philosophia tells Boethius of the "preoccupation of mortals" with "wealth, honours, power, glory, and voluptuous pleasures", she adds:

> diverso quidem calle procedit, sed ad unum tamen beatitudinis finem nititur pervenire.[70]

indeed this proceeds by diverse paths, and nonetheless it strives to arrive at the one goal, of felicity.

In "Petronius revived" this becomes:

Verumptamen quantumcumque se mulieres in concupiscentiis diversificent, ad unum tamen consummate scilicet luxurie finem solummodo tendunt.

However women diversify themselves in their desires, they nonetheless aspire only to arrive at the one goal, of consummated lust.

A moment later, the verse in "Petronius revived" mirrors that of the poem which immediately follows this prose passage in the *Consolation*. Boethius evokes the laws, the reins by which *(habenas . . . quibus)* mighty Nature *(Natura potens)* holds the vast orb in check;[71] for the twelfth-century Petronian it is holy Nature *(Natura . . . sancta)* who loosens, as well as curbs, the reins by which *(habenas . . . quibus)* happy relationships become venereal love.[72]

This author, whose mode of narration is seemingly amoral, was in this way inserting a piquant comparison between Petronian and Boethian values. Some of his first audience may well have recognised the echoes from the *Consolation,* and perceived the ironies that these created for the bitter erotic story they were hearing. Yet it is also possible that the author himself saw a connection between the two writers of *prosimetra,* Petronius and Boethius, which went beyond ironic juxtaposition of divergent world-views. That the link between the two runs deeper than this, that the majestic *Consolatio* reveals more than one glint of the irreverent *Satyricon,* is a suggestion I shall take further in the next chapter.

II

Allegory and the Mixed Form

At the opening of what survives of the *Satyricon*,[1] the narrator-protagonist, Encolpius, is making an impassioned harangue against the falsity and decadence of the professional *declamatores,* the rhetoricians and teachers of rhetoric, of his world. He invokes the great writers of the remote past, Sophocles, Euripides and the rest, and invokes an exalted ideal of purity of diction *(grandis et ut ita dicam pudica oratio),* in order to inveigh against the excesses, the sickness, not only of eloquence but of poetry and painting too, in his own time and place (2).

A moment later, Encolpius' speech is both interrupted and undermined. His critique of the rhetoricians had itself been a flood of rhetoric. An older man, a professional teacher called Agamemnon, does not let the young speaker "declaim" *(declamare)* any longer (3). Agamemnon cuts him short, though courteously, praising Encolpius' taste and love for a "good mind", and promises to let Encolpius in on the "secret art" of true eloquence. Yet this again turns out to be not what it claims. Agamemnon pays lip-service to the lofty, austere training of a golden past, but then insinuates the need for compromise if one is to keep any pupils at all: otherwise the teachers, "as Cicero says, 'will be left sitting alone in their lecture-rooms'" *(ut ait Cicero, "soli in scholis relinquentur").*[2] When Agamemnon launches into verses in praise of a modest and spontaneous style (5), his composition in fact becomes more and more stilted, and in the narrative that follows we are shown even more clearly that *this* Agamemnon, both academically and humanly, is a far cry from the grand name that he bears.

So, too, at the opening of Martianus Capella's *Marriage of Philology and Mercury (De nuptiis),*[3] a formally composed passage, that seems at first, like Encolpius' speech, to present a fixed position from which to proceed, reveals itself as vulnerable: it too is interrupted and ironically undermined. Here again an ostensibly straight piece turns out to be not quite what it seemed: it exists not in its own right but dramatically, as the first move in an interplay of minds and attitudes. The *De nuptiis* opens with an invocation to Hymenaeus, in which the god is allegorised as the principle and bond of cosmic love: Martianus' language here was to be drawn upon extensively by Boethius in his own poetic celebrations of "the love by which heaven is ruled".[4] Addressing Hymenaeus in elegiac couplets, the speaker at the start of the *De nuptiis* says:

> semina qui arcanis stringens pugnantia vinclis
>   complexuque sacro dissona nexa foves—
> namque elementa ligas vicibus mundumque maritas
>   atque auram mentis corporibus socias,
> foedere complacito sub quo natura iugatur,
>   sexus concilians et sub amore fidem . . .[5]

> Constraining the warring elements by mysterious chains,
> you cherish conjoined dissonances in a holy embrace:
> indeed you bind the elements in their exchanges, you impregnate
>   the world
> and unify the breath of mind with bodies,
> you under whom nature is yoked by an affectionate bond,
> you who bring harmony to the sexes and loyalty to love . . .

Who is the speaker of this imposing aretalogy? As soon as this is revealed, the verses themselves are called in question: they are deflated, relativised, seen as "an old man's frenzy". The hymn to the god of cosmic harmony is followed by a prose passage, which begins like this:

> Dum crebrius istos Hymenaei versiculos nescioquid inopinum intactumque moliens cano, respersum capillis albicantibus verticem incrementisque lustralibus decurvatum nugulas ineptas aggarrire non perferens, Martianus intervenit dicens "quid istud, mi pater, quod

nondum vulgata materie cantare deproperas, et ritu nictantis antistitis, priusquam fores aditumque reseraris, ὑμνολογίζεις?"[6]

While I was chanting these brief verses about Hymenaeus over and over, striving to compose something unexpected and untried, my son Martianus, unable to endure that I, my head sprinkled with white hairs and bowed by advancing years, should babble such unbefitting trivialities, interrupted me, saying: "What's all this, father? Why are you in such a hurry to sing when you haven't yet divulged the subject? You're hymnologising like a sleepy priest who starts his rite before opening up the portal and the sanctuary!"

Yet with this "correction" by the younger Martianus, we have not reached a fixed vantage-point either, any more than we had with Agamemnon's reply to Encolpius. Martianus senior, far from being a little ga-ga, as his son suggests, answers lucidly, giving as good as he gets:

"Ne tu" inquam "desipis admodumque perspicui operis ἐγέροιμον <non> noscens creperum sapis? nec liquet Hymenaeo praelibante disposita nuptias resultare? . . . fabellam tibi, quam Satura comminiscens hiemali pervigilio marcescentes mecum lucernas edocuit, ni prolixitas perculerit, explicabo".

"Are you so foolish", I said, "that you don't even dimly recognise the dawning of an illustrious work? Isn't it clear that, with Hymenaeus getting first bite of the feast set out, it is wedding-bells that are ringing? . . . I shall unfold for you a fable which Satura, devising in the long winter nights, taught the guttering lamps along with me— unless, that is, its length should disconcert you".

"Satura" here means not satire but the mixed dish of verse and prose, wittily personified; at the same time, the interchange reveals the essentially Menippean quality of undermining the seemingly fixed points of a discourse, of showing the testing and emerging of truth by way of ironically juxtaposed statements and attitudes, that are often themselves ironised in turn. The language, too, reflects this range of juxtapositions. The father, after his grandiose hymn, uses colloquial words self-mockingly *(nugulas ineptas aggarrire)*—to characterise his own composition as seen through his son's eyes. When his son uses a lofty-sounding Greek word, ὑμνολογίζεις—it appears indeed to be a nonce-word—sarcastically for his father's verse, Martianus in his reply turns to an equally recherché Greek term, ἐγέρσιμον—not I believe attested elsewhere as a noun[7]—to suggest the awakening of his *magnum opus*. Yet at once a hint of self-deflating irony returns: it's only something to while away the waking hours of the long winter nights; my Muse was not one of the sacred nine, but Satura.

Boethius was familiar with the *Satyricon* as with the *De nuptiis*: indeed one brief fragment of the *Satyricon* survives uniquely because Boethius cites it, at the close of his first commentary on Porphyry's *Isagoge*.[8] And I would suggest that the opening of *his "satura"*, the *Consolation of Philosophy*, is structured dramatically in the same way as the two passages I have cited from his predecessors. At first it might seem that all is not merely solemn but tragic:

> Carmina qui quondam studio florente peregi,
>   flebilis, heu, maestos cogor inire modos.
> Ecce mihi lacerae dictant scribenda Camenae
>   et veris elegi fletibus ora rigant.
> Has saltem nullus potuit pervincere terror
>   ne nostrum comites prosequerentur iter.
> Gloria felicis olim viridisque iuventae,
>   solantur maesti nunc mea fata senis.
> Venit enim properata malis inopina senectus
>   et dolor aetatem iussit inesse suam.
> Intempestivi funduntur vertice cani . . .[9]

> I who once composed songs fresh in their eagerness,
> weeping, alas, am forced towards mournful melodies.
> See how rending Muses dictate to me what I must write
> and elegiacs wet my face with veritable tears.
> At least no terror could prevent the Muses
> from following my path as my companions:
> they, once the glory of my blissful and green youth,
> now solace my fate—grieving old man that I am.
> For unexpectedly old age has come, hastened by ills,
> and sorrow has bidden its years to cling to mine.
> My hair is white before its time . . .

Boethius' language is that of his predecessors in Roman poetry—there are echoes of Vergil, Horace, Seneca, Prudentius, and most pertinently, of Ovid's elegies from his exile.[10] However deeply Boethius' sorrow during his imprisonment was rooted in his personal experience, is his *expression* of it here truly personal? Is it not a little affected and clichéd in its worn rhetorical devices—evoking not only the Muses but even such pallid quasi-personifications as *elegi, senectus,* and *dolor?* Precisely! In the prose that follows we learn that this is exactly what Philosophia feels about Boethius' lament. Scornfully, even ferociously, she claims that this lament was histrionic and false: she dismisses the Muses who had inspired Boethius here as "flighty little actresses"—"they get human minds used to their sickness and don't liberate them".[11] For the character Philosophia, those self-indulgent, derivative elegiacs do not represent the real nature of the character Boethius: they cannot do justice to what is finest in him.

The artistry of the opening verses lies not in themselves but in their contribution to a series of dramatic interactions: like Encolpius' tirade and Martianus' hymn (or, in a later period, like the *Monk's Tale,* or Chaucer's own *Sir Thopas,* in the *Canterbury Tales),* they are there to be shown as vulnerable, to be interrupted and undermined. Nor does the undermining itself provide a fixed point of repair: always the dialectic continues.

Before considering some aspects of Boethius' *Consolation* in more detail, I should like to pause at least briefly with two *prosimetra* that have had far less literary attention: the *Symposium* of the third-century Greek Father Methodius,[12] and the *De nuptiis* itself. Both of these include a substantial amount of verse that has been freshly composed, as well as snatches cited or adapted from earlier poets; both works likewise present a range of allegorical beings. And both reveal, I believe, a significant element of that Menippean mingling of earnest and game, that σπουδογέλοιον, by which serious insights are arrived at in ways more complex than the didactic, ways that never exclude the presence of unserious, playful perspectives.

Methodius' dialogue is a sacred parody of Plato's *Symposium:* instead of a group of men making speeches in praise of Eros, he presents a group of girls, each of whom makes a speech in praise of Purity (Ἁγνεία, Παρθενία). Methodius copies Plato's device of allegedly reporting the speeches at two removes: in his prelude, one girl, Euboulion, asks her friend Gregorion to relate what was said at the banquet of the ten maidens, at the invitation of Aretê, their hostess and arbitress. Yet it emerges from an aside that Gregorion had not herself been present, that what she is passing on is what she had learnt from Theopatra, one of the speakers. For the most part, however, Gregorion chooses to forget this, and to couch everything in words that imply she too had been an eye-witness and a guest. In the epilogue this ambiguity is given another, unexpected and witty, turn. There Euboulion says to her partner: "Tell me, the foreign girl from Telmessos (ἡ Τελμησσιακὴ ξένη), did she not listen, at least from outside?"[13] If, as Musurillo suggested, the allusion here is to Gregorion herself,[14] then her friend, by speaking of her thus in the third person, must be teasing her, saying in effect: Surely you must have eavesdropped, out of curiosity? Gregorion replies, sustaining the fiction and complicating it: "No—they say *that* girl was keeping Methodius company". This play with identities mirrors the play with multiple perspectives to be found in the course of the work, in which the girls' opinions about the nature of purity do not by any means always harmonise.

For Marcella, the first speaker, Parthenia is a being of ambiguous stature: "for one must suppose that, if she walks on the earth, her head touches the heavens" (Παρθενίαν γὰρ βαίνειν μὲν ἐπὶ γῆς, ἐπιψαύειν δὲ τῶν οὐρανῶν ἡγητέον).[15] This expression foreshadows that of Boethius about Philosophia.[16] So too in the next sentence, when Marcella says that Parthenia has had unworthy disciples, who desired her and were intent "only on possessing her", approaching her "in a vulgar way" (ὑπο βαναυσίας), I cannot help thinking of Philosophia's unworthy suitors in Boethius, the men who, in their possessive greed, tore violently at her dress, treating the sovereign lady as if she were a *meretrix*.[17]

Marcella's praise of Parthenia is followed by Theophila's speech. She argues that, however fine virginity may be, it is necessary for humans to increase and multiply. She even sees the moving outside himself (ἔκστασις) of Adam in his first sleep as a prefiguring of sexual joy.[18] Marcella interrupts her with an objection: What of the children born of adulterous loves—surely they cannot be willed by

God? Theophila in answer fashions an allegory inspired by Plato's myth of the Cave—here it becomes a round house, and then a womb, source of all life—in order to show that bastard children too are born innocent and good, and are divinely entrusted to guardian angels.

There are moments of both satire and invective scattered here and there in the work. In a brief interlude Euboulion complains how long the third speaker had been—what an ocean of words she had crossed! Her companion agrees, but says she must continue her narrative, lest she forget the other speeches, adding in what may well be improvised verses:

εὐεξάλειπτοι γὰρ νέων ἀκουσμάτων
μνῆμαι γερόντων.[19]

("For old people fail to remember even what they've newly heard"). As Gregorion is unmistakably a *young* woman, full of high spirits, the note of teasing irony in her verse is clear. There is a less lighthearted, more sardonic note in one of the speeches at the banquet, that of Thecla, particularly in her long polemic against the charlatanry of astrologers. It is Thecla to whom Aretê awards the supreme garland for her speech, and who, encircled by her companions, leads them in the wide-ranging, rapturous canticle of divine love—twenty-four strophes, from Alpha to Omega—in which she sings the verses and they answer with the refrain. In this, each of them becomes a figural fulfilment of the Wise Virgins of the parable:

Ἁγνεύω σοι καὶ λαμπάδας φαεσφόρους
κρατοῦσα, νυμφίε, ὑπαντάνω σοι.[20]

I keep myself for you, tending the shining lamps—
bridegroom, I come to you!

What is remarkable—and once more authentically Menippean—is that this sublime *psalmos* is followed by a prose epilogue filled with wit and gentle ironies. We are back with the narrator, Gregorion, and her friend, who asks her: "Who are the better? Those who feel no passionate desires, or those who master them?"[21] Gregorion is sure that the right answer is the first—so sure that she even proposes to instruct Euboulion about why this is so. Her friend is sceptical, and the argument continues in skirmishes of humorous, at times almost Socratic, raillery. "How wise you are!"—"I think you're making fun of me."—"No, I admire you . . . but the sages have found this question hard, whilst you not only know the answer but boast you can teach others." Gradually Euboulion gets the better of the argument, and the point of the juxtaposition of poetic canticle and prose epilogue becomes fully clear. Where the poetry evokes a mystic felicity, beyond all struggle, the complementary prose brings back—and praises—a more down-to-earth reality, the control of the passions. If Parthenia's head touches the heavens, her feet tread on the ground.

It is perhaps understandable that the traces of Menippean wit in Methodius should have gone unnoticed: one doesn't expect such things of a Church Father writing in praise of virginity. What is far more unexpected, and unfortunate, is that some recent scholars have likewise taken Martianus Minneus Felix Capella with relentless seriousness. Peter Parsons speaks of "Martianus Capella's straight-faced allegory";[22] Udo Kindermann goes so far as to claim that Martianus "shed all mockery and comedy, and alas shed also all the wit and spirit that had belonged to the Menippean genre before", in order to write "a deadly earnest encyclopaedia, overburdened by erudition".[23]

I hope the passage I have already cited, the altercation between Martianus and his son at the opening of the *fabella,* has begun to suggest otherwise. It is true that the *fabella* serves as a frame for the encyclopaedic parts of the *De nuptiis,* the seven long technical discourses by the maidens, the personified Liberal Arts, who are Philology's bridesmaids. And it is also true that these discourses—Books III to IX of the work—leave little room for verse, except for the opening and close of these books, or the epithalamium sung by Harmonia, the last of the bridesmaids to be summoned.[24] Yet even in the encyclopaedic books, when verses occur or are about to occur, Martianus shows himself gleefully aware of Menippean possibilities.

To mention only a few: Mercury cuts short Dialectica's lecture in Book IV, in verses where his impatience with her sophisms carries him away and leads him to more and more outrageous charges against the maiden: her deceitful spate of cumulative syllogisms "buzzes in the Thunderer's ears, a sin and a dreadful crime"; she is "a woman of shame . . . an indecent vagabond" (423); Rhetorica, at the close of her own lecture, "plants a noisy kiss on the top of the bride's head: for she never did anything quietly, even if she'd wanted to" (565); Voluptas, who, like Venus, is bored by the discourse of Geometria, interrupts it with verses mocking this maiden's uncouth looks (704):

> Hanc ego crediderim sentis spinescere membris
> neque hirta crura vellere;
> namque ita pulverea est agresti et robore fortis,
> iure ut credatur mascula.

> I'd have thought her limbs were spiky with thorns—
> no down on those bristly legs—
> she's so covered in dust, so like a brawny yokel,
> you'd think she was really a man!

It is again Voluptas who, dismayed at the prospect of yet another lecture, by Arithmetica, tries to seduce Mercury away from study by reminding him of the wedding-night to come: "Aren't these solemn commentaries dulling you, making you a limp husband? . . . What sort of hymeneal law is this? . . . Better for you to celebrate Priapus!" (725).

The longest of these interruptions is the Dionysiac episode (804 ff), in which the drunken Silenus, loudly belching, is slapped on his bald pate by Cupid. Martianus places this just when Astronomia's disquisition is expected. Thereupon Satura, his Muse, attacks him for his boisterous invention: "Felix, or Capella, or whatever your name is, with no more sense than the goat after which you're named, are you going out of your mind? . . . If you're not 'the ass hearing the lyre (ὄνος λύρας), know when's the proper time' . . . You'd rather be making up worthless farces than listening to the lecture of this star-speaking girl!"[25]

Philosophia was to rebuke Boethius with the same Greek maxim (ὄνος λύρας), taunting him with being insensible.[26] But where Boethius portrays himself as too despondent and cowed to answer back, the character Martianus, seizing on the fine poetic language of Satura, whose climax had come with the coinage "star-speaking" *(astriloqua),* mocks her in turn: "Bravo, my Satura! Has anger made a poet out of you?"

The Menippean ironies here work on two levels: on the one, both gods (Mercury and Venus) and allegorical beings (Voluptas) make fun of the book-learning of the seven maidens, and tell the reader with a wink that this can indeed become lengthy and wearisome, and is much less fun than sex; on the other, Satura, who had at the outset been claimed as the inspirer of the whole work, rebukes the author-character Martianus for his lack of seriousness, and gets herself lampooned. The irony deepens if we recall that the riotous *character* Martianus, an old man who suddenly, depicting Silenus, starts to behave like a Silenus, is none other than the earnest encyclopaedist. In the Menippean moments of the didactic books the author gives us glimpses of what we might call a meta-encyclopaedia, which is a joyous send-up of the encyclopaedia itself.

In the *fabella* of the wedding of Philology and Mercury, which is the theme of the first two books, Menippean techniques are used somewhat differently, as I should like to show by way of one brief illustration, from the initiation of the heroine, Philologia. Before she can marry in the heavenly world, Philologia must be "purged" of all her earthly learning. The goddess Immortality—Athanasia— "august of visage and resplendent with holy and ethereal light", tells her (135 f):

"Ni haec . . . coactissima egestione vomueris forasque diffuderis, immortalitatis sedem nullatenus obtinebis." At illa omni nisu magnaque vi quicquid intra pectus persenserat evomebat. Tunc vero illa nausea ac vomitio elaborata in omnigenum copias convertitur litterarum. Cernere erat, qui libri quantaque volumina, quot linguarum opera ex ore virginis diffluebant.

"Unless by violent retching you vomit all these things and bring them up, you'll never reach the seat of immortality." Philologia strained with a huge effort, and spewed up everything she had cherished in her heart. Then all that nausea and laboured puking turned into streams of literature of every kind. One could see what books, what immense volumes, works in how many languages flowed from the maiden's mouth.

As it all comes out, Philologia's literary spew is eagerly gathered up by the other maidens—the Arts, the Disciplines, the Muses. Then, since the heroine is weak with all her effort, Athanasia takes from her mother, Apotheosis, an egg which she gives Philologia to drink. This is her "draught of immortality" (141): it is the Orphic egg from which the universe was hatched,[27] it is an epitome of the cosmos in digestible form, which completes her initiation, and through which

> continuoque novo solidantur membra vigore,
> et gracilenta perit macies, vis terrea cedit
> aethereumque venit sine mortis legibus aevum.
>
> her limbs at once are made firm with new vigour,
> her ailing thinness passes, her earthly nature yields—
> an ethereal aeon, free from death's laws, draws near.

Martianus could be saying, like a mystic, that immortal knowledge is so different from mortal that the soul, to experience divine union, must void itself of all mortal knowledge first; or, like a satirist, that mortal knowledge is, in the last resort, mere regurgitation. Yet the total effect of the comic *via negativa* and initiation is exhilarating rather than simply mocking: Martianus gives an intimation of the grandeur of the underlying conceptions even while, by dwelling on them over-literally, he shows their grotesqueness and absurdity. In presenting mystical motifs, there is something Aristophanic about Martianus' technique—as when Aristophanes' Birds, vaunting themselves as the firstborn of creation, sing their version of the Orphic cosmogony:[28]

> There was no Earth.   No Heaven was.   But sable-wingèd Night
> laid her wind-egg there   in the boundless lap   of infinite Dark.
> And from that egg,   in the seasons' revolving,   Love was born,
> the graceful, the golden,   the whirlwind Love   on gleaming
>   wings.

And there in the waste   of Tartaros,   Love with Chaos lay
and hatched the Birds.   We come from Love.   Love brought us
   to the light.

Instead of unravelling the concepts abstractly, Martianus, like
Aristophanes, goes straight for a presentation that is exuberantly literal—and therein lies the element of mischief.

The *De nuptiis* comprehends a varied cast: the two human actors,
Martianus and his son, Satura, the Olympian gods, the Muses,
diverse kinds of spirits, and personifications: the heroine Philologia,
the seven Artes, Athanasia, Voluptas, and many others. The imaginative spectrum ranges from the most vivid and real to almost purely
rhetorical personifications. Yet even those that most tend towards
rhetorical figures or abstract concepts can come alive in what they
do: they are not static, they are given vitality through their movement in the narrative. As Marc-René Jung noted perceptively, if
each concept were defined once and for all, we could do without
allegorical narratives and reduce our texts to treatises.[29] Then Martianus' *prosimetrum* would be merely a discussion of the liberal arts,
that of Boethius a discussion of felicity and evil, free will and eternity—in each case with a certain amount of (superfluous) decora-
tion. But insofar as there is a *narratio,* to cite Marc-René Jung, "the
personifications elude tautology and become allegorical beings".
What arouses our curiosity as readers or listeners is the *manner* in
which they act: "The element that is new and unknown lies in the
manner".[30]

This is true in a more far-reaching way of Boethius' *Consolation,*
which not only features allegorical figures but is the first *prosimetrum,*
to my knowledge, where allegory plays a vital rôle in the whole
imaginative organisation of the work.

Boethius' heroine, Philosophia, is admittedly a learned construct;
there are many—almost too many—womanly or celestial beings in
earlier texts that help to account for aspects of her nature. In
Boethius' imagination there was the personified Wisdom, Hagia
Sophia, of the "Solomonic" books of the Old Testament—the
divine companion and helper in the creating of the cosmos, radiant

(candor lucis aeternae) and inspiring heavenly love in her devotee *(amator factus sum formae illius).*[31] Hagia Sophia was so far from being a merely rhetorical *façon de parler* that churches were built in her honour—the greatest of them, in Constantinople, by Constantine and his son. Again, Boethius knew the early Christian visionary allegory, the *Shepherd* of Hermas, where it is Ecclesia who appears as an old woman, radiantly dressed, carrying a book, who later becomes young and beautiful.[32] He knew of the goddess who had revealed philosophical truths to Parmenides, and who, like his own Philosophia, could sound stern to her disciple, as she incited him to more arduous intellectual efforts, and could also sound contemptuous of those incapable of reaching her own heights.[33] From Lucian's dialogue, *Fugitivi,* Boethius knew the personified Philosophia herself, the daughter who comes weeping to her father, Zeus. Lucian, like Boethius, recalls the death of Socrates as one of the greatest wrongs Philosophia had suffered, and like him too he insists that Philosophia is still being injured, even today, by coarse-minded pseudo-philosophers.[34] Perhaps, as I hinted, Boethius also recalled Methodius' figure Parthenia, whose head touches the heavens and who is pursued by vulgar men, bent only on fulfilling their desires; and most probably he knew the prosimetric opening of the *Mitologiae* of his near-contemporary Fulgentius, whose Muse, Calliope, finding him asleep, bursts into his chamber with contemptuous rebukes on her lips and an *ironicum lumen* in her splendid eyes.[35]

Thus it is not the features and details as such that are unparalleled in the case of Boethius' heroine: what is new and compelling lies in the way she behaves in the course of the dialogues, in the many-sided dramatic possibilities that are realised. As soon as Philosophia begins to speak, she takes on a life and personality of her own, she behaves vivaciously, temperamentally, unpredictably—not at all as we might expect of a personified abstraction. Her initial fierceness, as she drives off the "flighty little actresses" who had inspired Boethius' versified moan, shows a hint of amusement, but also of haughtiness, as she tells them: "if your blandishments had seduced some uncultivated fellow, I'd mind it less—that's common enough with you . . .—but *this* man, brought up on Eleatic and Platonic studies?"[36] In her arrogance, she is both protective and possessive: it's not as if he were a mere poet or actor—he belongs to *my* world, to *my* Muses.

When she turns to address Boethius himself, it is as his severe, sardonic doctor rather than as his beloved. Boethius shows the medical symptoms of the *lethargus*—speechlessness, numbness, loss of memory, glazed eyes. The wide-ranging, poetically coherent use of the imagery of sickness and healing throughout the *Consolatio* has been finely studied in an essay by Wolfgang Schmid.[37] The observation I should like to add to his concerns not the imagery itself but the changes of tone that go with it here at its first use. Philosophia begins aggressively, but then, with wry humour, speaks of Boethius in the third person, as if he couldn't hear her at all:

> Agnoscisne me? Quid taces? Pudore an stupore siluisti? Mallem pudore, sed te, ut video, stupor oppressit . . . Nihil . . . pericli est, lethargum patitur, communem illusarum mentium morbum. Sui paulisper oblitus est.[38]

> Do you recognise me? Why are you silent? Are you ashamed, or dazed? I wish you *were* ashamed, but I can see, a daze has overwhelmed you . . . There's no danger, he's suffering from a lethargy, a common disease of deluded minds. He's forgotten himself a little.

Yet her very next words—"He'll easily remember—if indeed he knew me before" *(Recordabitur facile, si quidem nos ante cognoverit)*— with their hint both of taunt and warning, show that Philosophia knows perfectly well that Boethius *can* hear her. And suddenly, to help him remember, she makes her first gesture of tenderness: "gathering her dress in a fold, she dried my eyes that were streaming with tears" *(oculosque meos fletibus undantes contracta in rugam veste siccavit)*.

Dramatically Philosophia is Boethius' intellectual guide, his spiritual healer, and his heavenly beloved. Is she also an aspect of his own consciousness? Jean de Meun, developing an idea of Abelard's, about how a human being can "consult his own reason, setting up himself and his reason as if they were two, like Boethius in his *Consolatio*",[39] claims that

Boeces establist et represente soi en partie de homme troublé et tour-
menté et demené par passions sensibles, et establist Philosophie en
partie de homme ellevé et ensuivant les biens entendibles. Si que en la
partie de soy il demonstre ses douleurs et les causes qui ses douleurs
esmeuvent, et en la partie de Philosophie il amene les causes qui
aneantissent ses douleurs . . .[40]

Boethius establishes and represents himself in the part of the human
being troubled and tormented and misled by sensible passions, and
establishes Philosophy in the part of the human being raised aloft and
pursuing intelligible goods. Thus in his own part he shows his griefs
and the reasons for them, and in the part of Philosophy he brings the
reasons that annihilate his griefs . . .

Jean de Meun's interpretation is valuable, provided we do not use
it reductively. It does not quite correspond to all that Boethius is
trying to convey. Beyond the dialogue between two aspects of himself, I think Boethius has the sense of receiving an illumination that
is almost more than human. In whatever mode the thoughts he
records came to him—whether the autobiographic substrate was
vision or dream, or simply meditation—Boethius believed passion-
ately in the truth of what was revealed to him. Thus his *revelatrix* is
no purely literary projection or topos: she is the ideal love of his
mind, the embodiment of all he could hope to know of truth on
earth, or (to put it more like Jean de Meun) the embodiment of all
that is finest in his own aspiring thoughts.

What is the rôle of the poetry in this many-textured composition?
Aspects of the answer have been given with beautiful insight in the
two essays, published posthumously after his tragically early death,
by Thomas F. Curley III.[41] To cite a few of his key sentences:

At times [the verse] serves to illustrate points made in the prose sections with the more vivid images of poetry . . . sometimes it actually
advances the argument . . . sometimes it is reserved for purposes less
appropriately treated in prose, namely, prayer . . . Finally, the effect of
the verse sections in the *Consolatio* is analogous in many ways to that
of the similes in the *Iliad* . . . [interjecting] aspects of reality not to be
encountered in the stark settings of the main action. In the *Iliad* . . .

the similes afford glimpses of the natural world of plants and animals, and of the workaday world of humans at their chores. Likewise in the *Consolatio,* all of which takes place within Boethius' prison cell, the verse sections continually present images of natural phenomena, both terrestrial and celestial . . .

Verse in the *Consolatio* functions as a "pharmakon", that is, as a potent substance of mysterious, almost magical, properties, which can either cure or kill.

Philosophia, as we have seen, stresses the danger lurking in Boethius' melancholy opening verses, verses which "get human minds used to their sickness and don't liberate them". The imagery of natural phenomena, however, has perhaps a more specific rôle than conjuring up the reality of the greater, open world whose life goes on beyond the prison. It is above all an elemental imagery, which provides a series of macrocosmic mirrors for the human soul:

> Nubibus atris
> condita nullum
> fundere possunt
> sidera lumen.
> Si mare volvens
> turbidus Auster
> misceat aestum,
> vitrea dudum
> parque serenis
> unda diebus
> mox resoluto
> sordida caeno
> visibus obstat . . .[42]

> Hidden in black
> clouds, the stars
> can pour out
> no light.
> If the turbid South wind
> whirling the sea
> stirs up the breakers,
> the wave that for long

was glassy and like
serene days
soon, grown murky
with loosened mud,
rebuffs our gaze . . .

Winds and stars, ocean and sky, sun and moon, night, dawn and day, recur in the poems over and over. They can be evoked for a likeness—their harmonies and disturbances can mirror what takes place in the human realm or the realm of the mind; but they can also be evoked for an unlikeness: elementally, all is a harmonious dance, with even the disturbances following a pattern of changes; only the human realm shows unpredictable discord and strife.

There is I think still another rôle for the poetry in the *Consolatio,* which Curley did not mention, and which I should like briefly to illustrate. The poetry is there at times in order to say what could scarcely be said any other way: poetic images can sometimes show what is beyond the power of prose statements to express.

Thus, before the conclusion of Book II, Philosophia brings her paradoxes about Fortuna to a point where she admits: "what I'm trying to say is something wondrous *(mirum),* and I can hardly explain my meaning in words".[43] Fortuna, she suggests, is true only when she shows herself unstable, in all her mutability; it is then that she frees human minds, with the knowledge of the frailty of felicity. In the prose, the *mirum* remains at the level of juggling with concepts and conundrums; in the poem that follows, Fortuna is perceived pointing beyond herself: by revealing mutability, she shows that mutability cannot be all there is, she shows (in Heraclitus' phrase) "an invisible harmony stronger than the visible", she shows a cosmos ruled not by mutability but by heavenly love:

Quod mundus stabili fide
concordes variat vices,
quod pugnantia semina
foedus perpetuum tenent . . .
hanc rerum seriem ligat
terras ac pelagus regens

et caelo imperitans amor.
Hic si frena remiserit,
quicquid nunc amat invicem
bellum continuo geret
et quam nunc socia fide
pulchris motibus incitant
certent solvere machinam . . .
O felix hominum genus,
si vestros animos amor
quo caelum regitur regat![44]

That the world with stable faith
varies its harmonious changes,
that the warring elements
keep a perpetual bond . . .
this cosmic order is bound
by the love that rules earth and sea
and holds sway over heaven.
If this love relaxed its reins,
all things that now love each other
would at once wage war,
strive to destroy the mechanism
which now they foster loyally
in beauty by their motions . . .
Oh happy race of humankind
if the love by which heaven is ruled
were to rule your minds!

In the images of cosmic harmony we perceive what the conceptual paradoxes could hardly begin to communicate: how Fortuna's world-view opens into Philosophia's.

At the centre of the *Consolatio* comes the poetic prayer *O qui perpetua,* which most medieval readers saw—I think rightly—as the focal point of the work, making it the chief object of their efforts at interpretation, sometimes devoting a full-scale commentary to this prayer alone.[45] Present-day scholars are more concerned than medieval ones with the historical questions: how far is this invocation a summary of Plato's *Timaeus,* how far does it include other elements in a philosophical synthesis?[46] I shall not touch on the cosmological details here, only try to define the way in which I think *O qui perpetua* is a *personal* synthesis, showing something that could not otherwise be said.

If we consider the petitions with which the prayer closes:

> Da, pater, augustam menti conscendere sedem,
> da fontem lustrare boni, da luce reperta
> in te conspicuos animi defigere visus.
> Dissice terrenae nebulas et pondera molis
> atque tuo splendore mica; tu namque serenum,
> tu requies tranquilla piis, te cernere finis,
> principium, vector, dux, semita, terminus idem.[47]

> Father, let my mind rise to your lofty throne,
> let me gaze on the fountain of good, let me, finding the light,
> fix the bright glances of the spirit in you.
> Scatter the mists and heaviness of my earthly mass
> and flash out in your splendour; for you are serene,
> you the calm rest for the holy—to see you is at once
> goal, start, mover, guide, pathway and end.

I find it hard to translate without putting in first-person pronouns, which are not in Boethius' text. The absence of such pronouns there is closely bound up with the poetic secret, the way in which Boethius and Philosophia are the same and not the same. Before the poem began, it was the character Boethius who had asked the character Philosophia to pray on his behalf; throughout *O qui perpetua*, she is voicing his thoughts for him. The prayers at the end are really Boethius' prayers—let *my* mind rise . . .—and yet, as Philosophia is speaking, the "my" and "me" are never uttered.

It is this polarity between the two characters that I should like to see dramatically, and to see as the distinctive achievement of Boethius the poet. In the earlier part of the prayer he is as it were saying through Philosophia the character: Intellectually I can grasp it all—in the abstract I know that the world is controlled in every aspect not by fickle Fortuna but by a divine guiding force, a creator "devoid of envy" *(livore carens)*.[48] Intellectually I can understand there is heavenly order behind the apparent injustice and chaos; but now—begs Boethius the character—let me perceive it visibly, let me know it personally, let my mind see it!

This is the essential theme of the *Consolatio*—a man trying to win *for himself* that insight into the divine principle present in the world, which he has been taught to accept since youth in the Neoplatonic schools. Can such an idealistic belief hold firm in a time of human crisis and despair? It is a question that can be as urgent today as it was in Boethius' prison-cell.

There are a number of Menippean moments in the *Consolatio:* the undermining of Boethius' elegiac verses at the opening, the testing of provocative ideas—that evil is nothing, that men who seem evil are mentally sick, and should be cured with compassion *(miseresce malis)*.[49] Yet the most deeply Menippean episode in the work, I suggest, is that of *O qui perpetua:* here, to cite once more from Bakhtin's definition, we see that "The menippea is a genre of 'ultimate questions'. In it ultimate philosophical positions are put to the test". As Menippus himself, in the fragment I cited, showed Diogenes, the philosopher sold as a slave, justifying his claim to be a master and not a slave,[50] so in the *Consolatio* we see how the dejected prisoner, seemingly weak, gains radiant strength.

The late eleventh century and the twelfth have left us four remarkable, very diverse, philosophical-allegorical *prosimetra,* by Hildebert of Lavardin (ca. 1097), Adelard of Bath (before 1116), Bernard Silvestris (1147), and Alan of Lille (ca. 1160–70).[51] All four works have literary links with the cathedral school of Tours.[52] None would have been conceivable without the intellectual and imaginative precedent of Boethius, and at least one of them—Bernard Silvestris' *Cosmographia*—develops the Boethian relations between poetry and prose in exciting new ways. The poetry at the opening of Bernard's cosmological fable is not introductory or elegiac: it plunges *in medias res,* evoking a moment of crisis in the drama of creation. The prose takes up the plot, the impassioned speech in the initial verses receives its answer in serenely built periods; then poetry once again grows out of the prose, developing luxuriantly what had been set down in lapidary formulations. At times the poetry recapitulates, but it as easily advances—not only to new ideas, but to new events in the *fabula.*

Each of these four allegorising *prosimetra* includes one or more feminine beings who are essentially Philosophia-figures—even when they are presented, as in Bernard Silvestris' *Cosmographia* or

Alan of Lille's *Complaint of Nature,* as goddesses or theophanies. In each work, too, there is what we might call a Fortuna-figure, a being who embodies mutability. She is called Philocosmia in Adelard of Bath's composition *(On Sameness and Difference),* Silva in Bernard's, Venus in Alan of Lille's. The relation between the Fortuna-figure and the "higher" figures untouched by change always has something enigmatic about it. These *prosimetra* could indeed be read as testings of that relationship (which may be dramatised in tensions, rivalries or conflicts)—as attempts to answer the question, is the lower, Fortuna-figure to be rejected, or must she be affirmed and seen as inseparable from her loftier counterparts?

Here I should like to focus briefly on the earliest and least known of these four compositions, Hildebert's "Philosophy of the Inner and Outer Human Being" *(Philosophia de interiore et exteriore homine),* as one of the early manuscripts I have used names it. It is still necessary to have recourse to manuscripts, since the text in the *Patrologia Latina* is badly garbled and there is no modern edition.[53]

Hildebert, before he came to Tours, had been bishop at Le Mans. There, in 1096 or soon after, as Fulco of Anjou and William Rufus fought for possession of the town, his episcopal palace had been ravaged by fire. The *prosimetrum* opens with a passage of seemingly autobiographical prose:

> Incendio domus mea corruerat, et reficiendi studio sollicitus hanelabam. Ligna cedi preceperam, quadrari, et expensas operi provideri. Totus eram in hoc et, omissis pontificalibus negotiis, quo in loco ponerem fundamenta, quantum palatia extenderem, nunc intuitu, nunc harundine metiebar. Quibus dum curiosus geometra insisterem, quedam ante occulos meos astitit, lugentis habitum gerens, et velut votum preter accidisset, similis conquerenti. Forma eius inenarrabilis, incognita magnitudo. Mira eius vivacitas, et quam crederes inmortalitatem polliceri. Vultus non semper idem: terram tristis, celos intuebatur hylarior. Celos ea tenerius respicere, celos desiderare et invita mecum morari videbatur. Ipsa quidem primo nive candidior apparuit, et regis apta complexibus; inestimabilem—sed precariam, sed aliunde sicut opinor adquisitam—preferebat venustatem. Dehinc autem quibusdam visa est squalere sordibus, quibus abluendis aquas esse necessarias minime dubitares. In manu eius libellus, in libello autem poeticum illud scriptum fuisse reminiscor:

Gaudeas an doleas, cupias metuasve, quid ad rem?

Obstupui, fateor, et quid diceret, quid ageret, sub silencio prestolari disposui. Tum illa: Miror, inquit, te sic oblitum mei . . .[54]

My house had collapsed in the blaze, and I was anxiously eager to cope with the task of rebuilding. I had ordered the timber to be cut and planed, the fees for the work to be released. I was wholly taken up with this, and, leaving episcopal business unattended, I was calculating the siting of the foundations and how far I could extend the palace, now by eye, now with a measuring-rod. While I, the fussing surveyor, was busy with all this, a woman dressed in mourning appeared before my eyes, like one lamenting, as if something unwelcome had occurred. Her beauty was ineffable, her height unparalleled, her vivacity amazing—you could imagine it giving promise of immortality. Her expression kept changing: she looked at the earth sadly, but more joyfully at the heavens: she seemed to gaze at the heavens more tenderly—to long for the heavens and to be unwilling to stop with me. At first she appeared more radiantly white than snow, worthy of a king's embrace; and yet her loveliness, in my view, though it was incomparable, was precarious, acquired rather than innate. And then she seemed to be sullied by some dirt—you could hardly doubt she needed water for washing it away. In her hand there was a book, and in the book I remember that a well-known verse was written:

> Whether you rejoice or grieve, or feel desire or fear, what does it matter?

I confess I was dumbfounded, and decided to wait silently to see what she would say, what she would do. Then she said: I am amazed that you have so forgotten me . . .

At first it all seems uncannily like the initial appearance of Philosophia in Boethius' *Consolatio.* Yet soon there are warning signals: this woman's beauty seems precarious and not really her own—and it's not that her dress has been torn, like Philosophia's, she just looks as though she needed a good wash.[55] There is a witty intertextuality here: Hildebert plays with his audience's Boethian expectations, but repeatedly undermines them. It might seem appropriate for a Boethian heroine to display a verse adapted from Horace's

Epistle *Nil admirari,* his celebration of philosophic calm;[56] yet soon we discover that this woman is anything but calm: she is excitable, full of passion and polemic. (I cannot help recalling that it is one of my most highly-strung friends who has hung the inscription "It doesn't matter" [*No importa*] above his desk.) Hildebert makes the process of recognising the apparition deliberately difficult, especially if one allows oneself to be misled by all the Philosophia connotations.

Here it is she who complains of feeling imprisoned, not the narrating "I", the counterpart of the captive Boethius. She reproaches Hildebert, the absorbed would-be architect, with finding her no appropriate guest-house in which to stay. She is bitter not only about the mean lodgings but that she, a *domina,* has there been humiliated like a slave: "my maidservant became a pimp and introduced ignoble lovers to me". Her accusations pass over into a *planctus* in verse:

> Quos igitur quadras lapides, que ligna secari
>   Precipis? in manibus virga quid ista facit?
> Quam suspiro domum non sculpto marmore surgit . . .[57]

> What are these stones you are squaring, what wood are you
> getting cut? What is this measuring-rod doing in your hands?
> The house I sigh for does not rise in sculpted marble . . .

Hildebert the character still does not know who his disdainful, querulous visitor might be; yet Hildebert the poet has already given many hints that she exists within him rather than outside him.

To humour her, he (the character) casts his measuring-rod aside and gives his workmen a long holiday.[58] She rebukes him for having forgotten her and his bond with her, and at last, in a plea heavy with Boethian echoes, the allegorical meaning is made patent even to the slow-witted Hildebert:

> Agno<s>cis eam que totum te implet, totum movet, totum regit et
> possidet? Agnosce, sodes, agnosce me . . .[59]

> Do you recognise her who fills you totally, moves you totally, rules
> and possesses you totally? Recognise, please recognise me! . . .

She is his *interior homo*—a part of himself, and someone responsible for him. She launches into accusing verses, that parody the poem in which Philosophia had lamented Boethius' numb dejection:

> Heu quam praecipiti mersa profundo
> mens hebet et propria luce relicta
> tendit in externas ire tenebras . . .[60]

> Alas how, drowned in a precipitous sea,
> his mind grows dull, forsaking its own light,
> and tries to move into the outer darkness . . .

She uses the identical metre and opening words—*Heu quam*—but turns the verses into brittle rhyming couplets:

> Heu quam turpe nefas, quam reprimendum,
> Quam discors anime, quamque pudendum![61]

> Alas how base a wrong, how needful to restrain,
> how alien to the soul, and how deserving shame!

In her vehemence she does not particularise, yet implicitly she must be charging *exterior homo*, Bishop Hildebert, with his absorption in worldly cares—in the restoration of his material palace to the detriment of his spiritual one.

He, however, turns the tables on his scornful opponent. The audience who knew how weakly poor Boethius had responded after Philosophia's outburst will have relished the irony of Hildebert's retort to this pseudo-Philosophia, whom he now understands as himself and can castigate as himself. He begins as if sympathising with her viewpoint, with three citations from St Paul about the spirit's longing to be free of its earthbound servitude. But when he brings up the Greek myth of Heracles, who dies tormented by his shirt of flame, he passes to the offensive. That shirt, he tells her, had been poisoned by another, but *you* administer your poisons yourself. All your boastings that you are the *domina* show merely that, if you accuse me, the guilt and the responsibility are yours.

The long reply of *interior homo,* in three passages of verse and two of prose, does not allow Hildebert to get in another word. He

appears to be overwhelmed by argument. His opponent now con-
fronts him with the seven powers of the soul (a set of distinctions
based on St Augustine's thought):[62] these, she claims, should over-
rule *exterior homo*'s cravings. The first power, *vivificatio*, he is told, is
especially loved by the flesh, that fears to die. Christ himself came to
earth in order to die, and still he prayed, "Let this cup pass from me".
If the flesh is too much molested, it can come to hate life and solicit
the spirit to suicide. Then the soul itself becomes fleshlike—like the
viper that strangles its own parents. Yet, *interior homo* concedes at last,
to turn one's back on life cannot be accomplished by the flesh alone,
only by a complicity and exchange of rôles: the work concludes with
the verses:

> . . . dum caro clamat, eamque
> Spiritus exaudit, consensu culpa creatur,
> Inque creando nefas, caro fit vir, spiritus uxor.[63]
>
> . . . when the flesh cries out and the spirit
> listens to it, guilt is created by complicity,
> and in creating wrong, flesh becomes husband, spirit wife.

There is something disconcerting about this close. The rôles of
the stronger and the weaker, to which we had become accustomed
as the allegory unfolded, are reversed, even grammatically: the feminine *caro* is now husband, the masculine *spiritus* wife. This could be
taken as just another ruse on the part of *interior homo*, by way of self-
defence, as if to say: in wrongdoing, you, the outer self, are the
powerful, tyrannous one, and I am helpless. Yet I would see something more far-reachingly ironic here. *Interior homo*, on her own
admission, has at last to climb down from the lofty attitudes she had
struck when she began. For in the last resort she knows she is no
Philosophia—she is bound to earth, for all her immortal longings.
She may think herself too good for *exterior homo*—whether we call
him the body or Bishop Hildebert. But ultimately she is aware that
her destiny lies with him—that, since she is his vivifier, his life is also
her life.

The cunning of Hildebert the artist lies in his staging the *ballo in
maschera* that prevents his composition from being a simple, sche-

matic debate of body and soul, such as we know from tenth-century Anglo-Saxon poetry[64] and from a host of later medieval poetic texts, Latin and vernacular. Here appearances are more deceptive. The "I" is at first Hildebert the character, the bishop sure of himself, the finicky designer giving orders to his builders. His interlocutor, tall and beautiful and dazzling, begins with all the air of being a projection as sublime as Boethius' heroine. The pretentions of both partners in the dialogue are undermined in the course of the work, and even the long concluding lecture by the "higher" figure reveals her ambiguity and her slipperiness. Both figures are, and are not, Hildebert.

In Hildebert's composition the occurrence of verse amid the prose seems to me less impelled by inner necessity than it is in Boethius. In the *Consolatio* we see precellently how the verse can communicate things beyond the ken of the prose. Yet I would also suggest that, in the *prosimetra* of both poets, the use of allegory is essential, not ornamental. It is what enables Boethius and Hildebert to show the iridescence of their inner search.

III

Narrative and the Mixed Form

When I was very young I was taken to a film called *A Song to Remember*—a life of Frédéric Chopin. If, after forty years and more, I recall it aright, it was a thoroughly romantic evocation of key moments in the composer's existence. The joy of first recognition in Paris, the excitement of being loved by George Sand, the gloom of sickness, the despair of being abandoned and near death: all these were presented as giving rise, at once and spontaneously, to some of Chopin's best-known compositions. No sooner had something cataclysmic happened to him than he was there at the piano, transforming it directly into a sonata or ballade, polonaise or étude. I remember wondering how all this exact information about what prompted Chopin's masterpieces was known, and my father explaining that a lot of it wasn't known at all, but was made up by the scriptwriter. Unwittingly I had stumbled upon one of the chief techniques by which "poets' sagas" had been constructed in Europe since archaic times.

As with composers, so with poets. People have seldom been content to see a poet's personality only as it is revealed in his or her poetry. There is an ancient and widespread craving to know more. What were those geniuses like in real life? What could they have lived through to make them compose as they did? In the surviving narratives that attempt to answer such questions, citing the poet's compositions by way of illustration and substantiation, doubtful and spurious attributions are often adduced as readily as authentic ones. Moreover, at every period certain stereotypes exercise a powerful influence on the narrators.

In the case of Homer, the principal stereotype is that of the begging-poet. The most gifted and brilliant of men is condemned to lead a lowly, precarious existence. Even if his wisdom, like his poetry, is marvelled at far and wide, still he must wander from place to place, and wherever he pauses to rest, he is at the mercy of people who may or may not give him food, lodging and means of subsistence. He bestows blessings on those who are generous to him, and he curses those who are arrogant or mean.

Homer features in two prosimetric poets' sagas which in their surviving form date from the second century A.D. One is a *Vita Homeri,* whose author, in order to lend his work high authority, claimed it was written by Herodotus.[1] As far as I can discover, this captivating *Vita* has received no translation, and little recent attention of any kind.[2] The other work, the anonymous *Certamen*—a poetic contest between Homer and Hesiod—is probably more familiar: it can be found bilingually along with Hesiod's works in the Loeb Classics.[3] Both the second-century authors were using materials that had been assembled from popular traditions some six centuries earlier, and one motif that they share—a children's riddle which Homer fails to solve—is demonstrably older still: it was already cited and expounded by Heraclitus.[4] At times the two second-century writers take an almost folkloristic stance, collating variant versions of details and of episodes.

According to Pseudo-Herodotus, Homer was born in Smyrna, the illegitimate child of a girl Cretheïs. She named him Melesigenes—the son of the river Meles, where she bore him. (He does not get the name "Homeros" till, as an adult, he has gone blind, and is rejected by the people of Cymê, whose word for "blind man", the author assures, was "Homeros".) Cretheïs takes work in the house of a teacher, Phemios, to pay for her child's education, and then agrees to marry Phemios, for the boy's sake. The young Homer excels in learning, and grows up to inherit Phemios' school. Merchants who sail to Smyrna from afar come to spend their free evenings there, listening to him spellbound. One of them, a sea-captain called Mentes, persuades Homer to disband the school and go with him to see the world. In Ithaca, where Homer's eye-disease begins, compelling him to a longer stay, he learns all about the traditions of Odysseus, in the house of Mentor, his kindly host. The *Vita* continues as an account of Homer's wanderings. It is poverty that forces him, having lost his sight totally, to travel over and over again. His first verses are begging-verses at Neonteichos, where a compassionate cobbler, Tychios, gives him lodging. Homer earns his living there composing poetry—his *Thebaid* and his *Hymns*—and all are amazed at his verses and wisdom.

In the next town, Cymê, Homer offers the citizens a bargain: he will make them illustriously remembered, on condition that they provide means for him to live. The city council, by a narrow margin, votes against the proposal, and Homer leaves, having composed a curse upon the Cymaeans: in their land no poet shall ever arise who will give them fame. After other episodes (such as that of the dishonest schoolmaster, Thestorides, who writes down Homer's epics and then travels, trying to pass them off as his own), Homer settles on the island of Chios, where he founds a school for poetry, marries, and has two daughters.

He commemorates those who had helped him in the past, immortalising them by working their names into his poetry: his teacher Phemios and his hosts Mentes and Mentor into the *Odyssey,* the helpful cobbler Tychios into the *Iliad*—always the author of the *Vita* cites the appropriate verses in support. Before going to Athens, Homer inserts verses extolling Athens into his *Iliad*. As he approaches the city, however, some women are sacrificing to the goddess Kourotrophos, in order to bear children, and the priestess drives the blind poet away. Homer retorts with the improvised verses:

Κλῦθι μοι εὐχομένωι Κουροτρόφε, δὸς δὲ γυναῖκα
τήνδε νέων μὲν ἀνήνασθαι φιλότητα καὶ εὐνήν,
ἣ δ' ἐπιτερπέσθω πολιοκροτάφοισι γέρουσιν,
ὧν ὥρη μὲν ἀπήμβλυνται, θυμὸς δὲ μενοινᾶι.

Kourotrophos, hear my prayer! Grant that this woman
shall henceforth scorn the love and the bed of young men!
Let her delight just in old men, grey at the temples,
whose potency is dulled and who keep only their lust! (30)

In Athens, too, when potters ask Homer for a blessing on their work, his reply has all the marks of a two-edged begging-poem. If the potters reward the *vates,* he will call upon Athena to guard their kiln with her protecting hands; but if they try to cheat him, he'll call upon a rout of destructive sprites and poltergeists, to make the kiln explode and singe the face of any potter who goes near it (32).

At Samos, Homer is said to have composed, for the children who guided him, the "swallow-song" with which, once a year, they go in procession from door to door, invoking blessings and begging for gifts. In the version in the *Vita* the children do this without threats: it is in the more celebrated swallow-song, recorded by Athenaeus, that they likewise conjure up what will happen if their pleas are rejected: "We'll carry your door away, or your lintel, or the woman who's sitting inside . . ."[5]

The power of the legendary poet who is also a beggar is recognised in many societies.[6] Not only can he give undying fame to those who treat him well, but as *vates* he can be a society's special link with the divine realm, whose powers he can harness, for good or ill. Already in hymns of the *Rigveda,* the formation of which reaches back into the second millennium B.C., such a *vates* appears not just as a brahman priest but as a wandering minstrel who asks for gifts. In the spirit of reciprocity, the poet presents himself not as if he were begging for alms but as if he were himself bestowing gifts, through his blessings. In one hymn (*Rigveda* I 125), the speaker evokes the figure of the bard as he comes to the house of a wealthy host:

1. At dawn the guest who comes at dawn brings a jewel.
    The enlightened man who lodges him adds to his treasure.
    Through him such a man increases his progeny and life-
       force . . .

6. Beautiful things are only for those who give the singer's
       reward,
    the suns in the heavens shine for those who give the singer's
       reward,
    they enjoy the substance of immortality, they who give the
       singer's reward . . .

7. . . . Sorrows shall strike the man who is miserly![7]

The poet we encounter in the *Vita Homeri,* blessing and cursing, asking for sustenance and granting immortality, exemplifies the same archetype.

The rôle of the verses in the pseudo-Herodotean *Vita* is manifold: we see Homer improvising begging-poems, panegyrics, prayers and invocations, benedictions and maledictions, prophecies and warnings; an epitaph, a propempticon, and a children's song, as well as lines commemorating his friends, for inclusion in the *Iliad* and the *Odyssey.* All are presented as composed on the spur of the moment:[8] like Chopin in the film from my childhood, Homer is always shown creating *A Song to Remember.*

In the *Certamen,* Homer is portrayed as excelling in still other ranges of poetry: the enigmatic and the gnomic. The author has something of the antiquarian about him: after comparing various biographical traditions about Homer and Hesiod, he fastens on one that showed them as contemporaries and rivals. For their contest he provides a prose frame, a kind of narrative continuo; the two poets, however, speak entirely in hexameters. Their *agôn* comprises several stages, each of which is a test of wisdom and wit. The poet as *vates* must display instant mastery of whatever knowledge is required of him. There is a mythological counterpart to such a poetic testing in the Norse Eddic lay *Vafþrúðnismál,*[9] where Óðinn, god of poets and poetry, matches his knowledge and shrewdness against that of the giant Vafþrúðnir, as they question and answer each other in a series of alternating strophes. In the light of the Homeric tradition, it seems to me of particular interest that when Óðinn first goes to the giant it is in the guise of a begging-poet:

> I have come from my wandering,
> thirsty, to your hall,
> in need of hospitality
> and of your welcome—
> I have travelled long . . . (8)

Óðinn even calls himself "a poor man who has come to the rich" (10).

In the *Certamen,* Hesiod begins by asking Homer, in verse, what is best for mankind, and what is most delightful. Angered at the felicity of his opponent's replies, Hesiod challenges him anew, with a conundrum: to sing the things that neither are nor were nor shall be. With ready wit Homer rises to this seemingly impossible task. Then Hesiod asks Homer to complete hexameters of his own which, taken in themselves, are of doubtful meaning or nonsensical: each time, Homer at once finds a complementary verse that makes or restores sense. So for instance he caps Hesiod's line:

ὣς οἳ μὲν δαίνυντο πανήμεροι οὐδὲν ἔχοντες

Thus they feasted all day long, having nothing

with

οἴκοθεν, ἀλλὰ παρεῖχεν ἄναξ ἀνδρῶν 'Αγαμέμνων.

from their own homes, as Agamemnon, lord of men, provided.[10]

Next, after a mathematical riddle, come nine further questions of Hesiod's, probing the nature of the good life. Homer answers each in lapidary gnomic verses. Finally, the king Paneides, who is the judge of the contest, asks each poet to recite the most beautiful passage from his own works. The populace acclaim Homer as the victor, but the king overrules them, saying the garland must go to Hesiod—to the poet of peace, and not the poet of war.

Both the *Vita* and the *Certamen* contain memorable moments, and a number of verses not unworthy of the legendary poets to whom they are ascribed. Yet both works become increasingly ragged in structure near their close. It is as if the second-century authors, or redactors, wanted to cram in all the traditions concerning these poets that they had garnered. Both works, when they come to treat Homer's death, include the riddle of the boys who had gone fishing:

ἅσσ' ἕλομεν λιπόμεσθα· ἃ δ' οὐχ ἕλομεν φερόμεσθα.

All that we caught we leave behind; what we did not catch, we carry with us.[11]

It is the one and only riddle that the consummately wise and canny poet is unable to resolve. The answer—which the children proceed to tell him—is a comic one: they had caught not fish but lice, leaving those they caught on the shore, but still carrying on their bodies those they couldn't catch. The author of the *Vita* knows, but rejects, a tradition that Homer died of chagrin at his failure to find the answer; in the *Certamen,* more impressively, the riddle was prefigured at the outset: the Pythian oracle had intimated that a children's riddle would betoken Homer's death.[12] This suggests to me that the riddle may originally have borne a meaning symbolically related to that death, one which goes beyond the verbal trick that the children play upon the poet. The wording of the riddle in Heraclitus[13] strongly suggests this more serious aspect: "Whatever we saw and grasped, we leave behind; whatever we neither saw nor grasped, we carry with us." Here the way of stating the paradox seems to match perfectly the destiny of the supreme begging-poet: having possessed in life none of the visible or tangible things that must be left behind, he carries with him into death his invisible, intangible renown.[14]

Another kind of poet's saga, treating the life and compositions of a love-poet, works with a very different kind of stereotype. In at least three medieval vernaculars—Irish, Icelandic, and Provençal—we have prose narratives that cite the strophes of love-poets to the women they loved. And the point of the narrative is always that for some reason the poet as lover is deluded in his hope of full possession, or lasting enjoyment, of the beloved. In the stories it is as if the poet's inspiration could only remain fecund if there was no chance of their living together in happy union.

It is true that, when a poet addresses loving strophes directly to a woman, in the ancient and medieval poetry known to me, he does not often dwell on consummation or the bliss of possession. These are more likely to be mentioned in poetry with a narrative aspect (such as dawn-songs in the sphere of lyrical poetry)—or again, in verses in a satiric register. On the other hand, the strophes addressed to a longed-for beloved, who is not depicted as yielding fully, acted as a spur to the tellers of poets' sagas: from ardent strophes that do not mention yielding, they could elaborate reasons for that unyieldingness; they could invent freely the narrative situations in which those verses might first have been uttered; but they could also return to the verses and use these as *auctoritates* for their free inventions.

If the love-poet's situation—fervent but frustrated—is portrayed similarly in a number of poets' sagas in the three vernacular traditions, the relations between prose and verse in these portrayals are extremely varied.

Chronologically the earliest is the Irish tale of the poet-lovers, the woman Liadain and the man Curithir, which its editor, Kuno Meyer, dated on linguistic grounds to the ninth or early tenth century.[15] The complete text, prose and verse, comprises only eight pages in Meyer's edition. It includes just under a hundred lines of verse, in rhyming quatrains and tercets. The story appears to play in a more ancient epoch: the lovers seek the spiritual guidance of Cummine, son of Fiachna—a saint known to have died in the year 662.[16] It is difficult to ascertain whether any of the verses attributed to Liadain or Curithir in the saga could go back to so archaic a period; at the same time, one can hardly suppose that the saga as we have it could be the work of a single author, who composed both the prose frame and the love-poetry. For the prose is disappointingly sketchy, and, in certain vital narrative details, quite baffling. To cite Meyer:

> It was evidently the chief object of the writer to preserve the quatrains [and tercets], and to let his prose serve merely as a slight framework in which to set the poetry.[17]

That is, he was preserving lyrical love-poetry of great power, which an older oral tradition had attributed to the poets Liadain and Curithir.[18] He may have been assuming that an audience would know the basic outline of what had happened to the pair well enough to need only swift, allusive reminders from the teller; or again, that any teller would have to be word-perfect in the verses, but would require, for the framing narrative, only a few succinct notes, which he could elaborate ad lib; or finally the writer could have left certain elements in the narrative deliberately cryptic, challenging his public to "Peece out our imperfections with your thoughts". It may be significant that the allusions in the poetry, especially to Liadain's and Curithir's physical love, are likewise cryptic: quite possibly the narrator, like his poetic sources, wanted to shroud the details of this in mystery and delicacy.

When Liadain visits Connaught, as a wandering poet, both she and Curithir, her host, are already renowned for their poetic compositions. She promises Curithir that she will reward his proffered love if he comes to visit her in turn. When a poet-fool, Mac Da Cherda, at Liadain's court, announces Curithir's arrival, he does so in five riddling quatrains, one of which intimates that she has cheated her wooer and taken vows as a nun.[19] Notwithstanding those vows, Liadain goes with Curithir; but then, filled with guilt, they submit themselves to St Cummine's spiritual direction. He devises for them a penance such that Liadain and Curithir can still hear, though not see, each other—and thus they both compose their loving quatrains, lamenting their physical separation. On one night, when the saint allows them the test of lying together but without making love,[20] they transgress, and Curithir is sent away. The high point of the saga is Liadain's lament that then follows—ten three-line strophes grieving that she had brought sorrow to Curithir, her incomparable love:

> Cen áinius
> in gním í do-rigénus:
> an ro·carus ro·cráidius.
>
> Ba mire
> nád dernad a airersom,
> mainbed omun Ríg nime . . .
>
> Mé Líadan,
> ro carussa Cuirithir:
> is firithir ad-fíadar . . .
>
> Ní chela:
> ba hésium mo chrideṡerc,
> cía no carainn cách chena.
>
> Deilm ndega
> ro thethainn mo chridese;
> ro-fess, nicon bía cena.

Joyless
the deed I have done:
when I have loved I have tormented.

It would be madness
not to do what he desired,
were it not for fear of the King of heaven . . .

I am Liadain,
I have loved Curithir:
it is only too true, what is said . . .

Do not hide it:
he was my heart's love,
even were I to love all others.

A roaring flame
has split my heart:
without him surely it will not survive.[21]

Liadain's loving but enigmatic *planctus* must have set problems for storytellers whose audiences longed to know what had really happened to the author of this lament—or to the character projected in it. What was the mystery of her guilt? That she played Curithir false by becoming a nun before he arrived to claim her promised love?[22] That she slept with him nonetheless? That she failed St Cummine's test of married chastity? Or had she in fact flirted with other men ("he was my heart's love,/even were I to love all others")? Or again, was she a prototype of the kind of girl that would one day, in a ballad, be named Barbara Allen—a girl who only really feels love when it's too late to show it? It is as if the *planctus,* and the preceding verses of both lovers, had confronted the storyteller with too many possible motivations. His narrative is obscure partly because it is over-laconic; but perhaps it is also over-laconic because the teller did not know how to choose one unequivocal story-line.

The saga of the Icelandic poet Kormakr[23] presents a similar problem of a plethora of possible motivations—but here the problems of the relation between the verses and the prose are complex too. We have, however, the benefit of a meticulous recent study of these in a book by Heather O'Donoghue.[24]

Kormakr is a historical figure in tenth-century Iceland. Some of his panegyric verses to an earl of Norway are preserved outside his saga, as is a couplet addressed to þorkell, the man who, in the saga, is the father of his beloved Steingerðr. The saga itself was written, according to its editor, Einar Ólafur Sveinsson, in the early thirteenth century. Among the eighty-five strophes of skaldic verse that it includes, three quarters are ascribed to Kormakr. Some thirty-five of these are addressed directly to Steingerðr, or show him reflecting upon his love for her; others represent Kormakr's responses—defiance, mockery, self-justification, boasting—in various situations that arose on account of his love. From the saga it seems that this "love is of a birth so rare" as that of Liadain and Curithir; again the wellspring of the poetry appears to lie in the erotic frustration. Kormakr falls in love at first sight, or strictly, even before first sight: he is filled with awe and foreboding as he glimpses Steingerðr's beautiful ankles, and is overcome by undying love a moment later, as he sees her radiant eyes. The events that follow are as preposterous as any in the Greek romances: in brief, Kormakr woos and is betrothed to Steingerðr, but does not turn up at his wedding. Steingerðr marries another man, then rejects her first husband and marries a second, and each time her marriage spurs Kormakr to outbursts of renewed ardour for her. At times she welcomes his fervid behaviour, at others she is angered by it. Kormakr derides and makes grim fun of both her husbands in his verses, and challenges them to sword-fights; at last, when Kormakr rescues Steingerðr from pirates, and her second husband, þorvaldr, offers to relinquish her, so that she can go with her deliverer, Steingerðr sourly refuses to "swop knives", and the poet agrees that he and she were fated never to be one.

In the past there has been dispute over whether the love-verses—many of which show a distinctive and exciting poetic gift—could stem from the historical Kormakr, or at least stem from the tenth century, or whether they are later compositions, collected or even invented by the saga author. From a philological analysis of the verses ascribed to Kormakr (especially of metrical features, choice of idioms, and word-forms), Einar Ólafur concluded that "marks of antiquity... indicate that the greater part date back to the tenth century. However, many of them are clearly very corrupt."[25] Before the time of the saga writer, that is, such verses had become garbled in oral tradition, and had seen attempts by generations of reciters to complete, correct and refurbish them. Some verses, again, were probably invented wholly afresh after the tenth century, though Einar Ólafur thinks it unlikely that the saga-writer himself was competent to continue such invention.

What is fascinating in the saga is not only Kormakr's poetry but its many-sided relation to the prose. Thus for instance, near the opening, where the prose author presents Kormakr's love-verses as his spontaneous reaction to the first sight of Steingerðr, O'Donoghue notes that there are past and future tenses in the poetry, which show it to be a blend of retrospection, immediacy, and prophetic foreboding, unmistakably composed *after* the events.[26] It is emotion recollected, even if not in tranquillity:

> Brunnu beggja kinna
> bjǫrt ljós á mik drósar,
> oss hlœgir þat eigi,
> eldhúss of við felldan;
> enn til ǫkkla svanna
> ítrvaxins gatk líta,
> þró muna oss of ævi
> eldask, hjá þreskeldi.

> Brámáni skein brúna
> brims und ljósum himni
> Hristar hǫrvi glæstrar
> haukfránn á mik lauka;
> en sá geisli sýslir
> síðan gullmens Fríðar
> hvarmatungls ok hringa
> Hlínar óþurft mína.

> Bright torches from both cheeks
> of the girl blazed at me
> —laughter chokes in my throat—
> over the kitchen's panels,
> and more, I glimpsed the lovely
> ankles by the threshold:

the longing will not grow old
for me as long as I live!

The eyelashes' moon, under the eyebrows'
bright heaven, hawk-gleaming,
shone upon me from the linen-lustrous
lady of the leek's brine;
and that moonbeam from the eyelids
of the gold-necklaced goddess
now works, for that Hlín of rings,[27]
her ruin and my own.

I have chosen to cite Kormakr's second and third strophes, to suggest the extremes of vividness and verbal complexity, of concreteness and fantasy, of exalted and lowly allusion, that characterise the finest strophes attributed to him. The prose author, trying to present these as what Kormakr said on the spur of the moment when he first experienced Steingerðr's presence, cannot take account of the subtle transitions of tenses in his source.

There are sections of the saga where the verses, in O'Donoghue's words, "outshine a flat, even bathetic, prose", or where the prose "is evidently no more than a minimal framework to accommodate the verses", or again where "the prose author inherited two separate incidents, each commemorated by the same verse".[28] At times he is, it would seem deliberately, unselective, including more material relating to Kormakr than he could accommodate structurally—in case certain traditions should become lost. There are also verses which could hardly have survived without accompanying explanatory prose, and yet these include some where the extant prose is obscure or inadequate: such verses must have had earlier, more coherent narrative settings.[29] Towards the end of the saga the author has collected "the flotsam and jetsam of traditional material" about his protagonists, creating "from innumerable different stages" in the traditions about them.[30] In this his procedure seems to me similar to that of the authors of the *Vita Homeri* and *Certamen,* as they approach the close of their confections.

I would suggest that, perhaps already soon after the year 1000, another generation was curious as to what really lay behind the haunting verses of Kormakr for Steingerðr. They would have asked their parents or grandparents, "If he loved her so much, why did they never get married?" And the answers, based on rumour and anecdote, and at times a gift for artistic embellishment, will have varied. Some will have said: "It was because a witch laid a curse on Kormakr"; others, "As he was of noble birth, Kormakr thought himself too grand to wed her—but how he regretted it afterwards!"; others again, "The two families had a quarrel over the dowry"; still others, "Kormakr was a strange man: he was obsessed with the pursuit of Steingerðr, but lost interest as soon as fulfilment was possible". Now all these four "explanations" that I have just paraphrased are slipped in at various stages of the saga by the thirteenth-century author. This was, I believe, because he had inherited all of them, and, like a contortionist, he tried to take cognizance of them all. He does not have the more antiquarian outlook—"some say this, and some say that"—of the Greek writers about Homer and Hesiod, nor, like the narrator of *Liadain and Curithir,* does he simply cut off when the problems get too deep for him; rather, he insinuates the incompatible motives and explanations as if they were all compatible.

When we turn to the nearest equivalent to poets' sagas in Provence, the relation between poetry and prose is far simpler. Here there is no question of a long oral tradition bridging the gap between the verses and the prose narratives: on the whole, what we have in Provençal are brief prose pieces elaborating on lyrics composed only a few decades earlier;[31] in one case, the prose narrator, who names himself, even tells that he knew the poet personally and acted as his messenger in love.[32]

The Provençal narratives have been mentioned in connection with the Icelandic poets' sagas,[33] but without a clear perception of the marked differences between the materials that survive in the two traditions. First, the difference of scale. *Kormaks Saga* fills a hundred pages in the critical edition; other Icelandic sagas about poets, such as those of Hallfreðr and Gunnlaugr, are of comparable size. In complete contrast, three pages is the maximum length of any one narrative about a troubadour and his songs—amatory, topical or satirical—among a hundred and sixty or so extant texts of this kind.[34]

The texts about troubadours and their poetry consist of "lives" *(vidas),* and "commentaries" *(razos)* on individual lyrics. There are just over a hundred *vidas* preserved, though only a handful are of any interest in relation to poets' sagas: for the great majority are minute (ranging from two lines of prose to about twenty), and it is relatively rare for them to cite any poetry. More promising are the sixty or so *razos.*[35] These are accounts of how certain lyrics (by eighteen different troubadours) came to be composed—accounts in the exact sense of the film from my childhood, *A Song to Remember:* biographical short stories, rich in citation, explaining the immediate circumstances in which a song arose. Mostly *razos* comment on only one song (just occasionally they extend to two or more). Some troubadours were given a number of discrete *razos,* for diverse songs: the colourful, bellicose Bertran de Born far outstrips all others, with no fewer than eighteen *razos.*

While some of the troubadour *vidas* stem from the late thirteenth or fourteenth century, nearly all the extant *razos* were in existence by 1219, and were probably redacted, or written up, in the preceding decade by a single author, the troubadour Uc de San Circ, who also subsequently, in the period after 1231, added a group of *vidas* to them.[36]

Uc's collection includes some memorable anecdotes, vivaciously told. I should like to pause with the celebrated account, in a *vida* and two *razos,* of the life and songs of Peire Vidal.[37] Many of the features of Peire's life, as recorded there, are wildly fantastic, yet various scholars have been able to show, for separate details, that these are not freely invented, but draw upon verses by or about this troubadour. They have explained the fantasies as misinterpretations of the poetry, and this is convincing as far as it goes. Yet I would suggest that one must go further: in the case of Peire Vidal, there seem to me to be suspiciously many such "misunderstandings", and each of them gives rise to such outrageous pieces of narrative that I believe the "misunderstandings" are both willed and mischievous. That is, I think Uc de San Circ deliberately took a group of metaphors and hyperboles in the poetry literally in order to present a portrait that is sensational in content and satiric in tone. Read as satire of the more extravagant aspects of troubadour diction, the extraordinary misconstructions that have troubled historically-minded scholars take on coherence and sense.

The *vida* tells that Peire, son of a furrier in Toulouse, was one of the craziest men who ever lived *(dels plus fols omes que mais fossen)*. It was true, says Uc, that a knight of Saint-Gilles cut Peire's tongue, for having insinuated that he was the lover of the knight's wife. (A prince, Uc del Bauz, saw to it that Peire was treated and healed.) This incident seems to be extrapolated from a strophe devoted to Peire in a lyrical invective *(sirventes)* of 1195 by the Monk of Montaudon, who makes fun of a series of sixteen troubadours (including himself):

> Peire Vidals es dels derriers,
> Que non a sos membres entiers;
> Et agra·il ops lenga d'argen
> Al vilan qu'era pelliciers,
> Que anc, puois si fetz cavaliers,
> Non ac puois membransa ni sen.[38]

> Peire Vidal's among the last—
> not all his limbs are sound;
> he'll need a silver tongue,
> that base-born furrier,
> who, since he made himself a knight,
> has neither memory nor sense.

Avalle, Peire's excellent editor, claims that the biographer's misunderstanding of this strophe seems so improbable that the tongue-cutting incident is likely to have a quite different, but untraceable, source.[39] I agree that it *is* improbable—but would add, deliberately so.

In Cyprus, the *vida* continues, Peire married a Greek girl, "and people gave him to understand she was the niece of the Emperor of Constantinople, and that he should rightfully have the Empire because of her. So Peire spent all he could earn on building ships, for he thought to go and conquer the Empire. And he bore imperial arms and had himself called 'Emperor' and his wife 'Empress'".

It is true that many of Peire's songs show his weakness for hyperbole, and that *emperial* (in the sense of "lofty") and *emperador* are

among his favourite words[40] (ones for which indeed another troubadour once mocked him).[41] In a love-song, for instance, Peire says: "I
am crowned with exalted joy / more than any emperor".[42] In this
song, which is addressed to a lady called Loba, Peire's asseverations
have a potentially farcical aspect. Playing on the etymology of Loba's
name (she-wolf), he affirms that

> E sitot lop m'appellatz,
> No m'o tenh a deshonor,
> Ni se·m baton li pastor,
> Ni se·m sui per lor cassatz.[43]

> Even if you call me "wolf"
> I don't hold it a dishonour—
> even if the shepherds beat me
> and they give me chase.

How would the shepherds have known if Loba called the poet her
"wolf"? Uc in his *razo* gave the inspired answer: Peire must have disguised himself in a wolfskin. From there—with the help of the
song—it was but a step to his legend (recreated poetically in our
century by Ezra Pound): the shepherds, taking this disguised creature
for a real wolf, hunted the troubadour, beat him and left him for
dead at Loba's lodging.[44]

Finally, an allusion to a stolen kiss, repeated in several of Peire's
songs, gives Uc the pretext for a highly dramatic—but I think evidently humorous—*razo*.[45] It is noteworthy that Kormakr, too, has a
strophe about stolen kisses, and that the saga-writer includes in his
narrative two separate incidents when Kormakr is said to have
responded with that strophe.[46] Before one is tempted to the suggestion that the Icelandic author is indebted to Uc de San Circ for the
motif, or that the strophe attributed to Kormakr must stem from the
thirteenth century, it is as well to observe the differences between
the accounts. Kormakr on two occasions is said to kiss Steingerðr in
public, in the presence of Þorvaldr, her second husband, in order to
mock and humiliate him; Peire, on the other hand, creeps into the
bedroom of Azalaïs, when her husband Barral, Lord of Marseille, has
left. Steingerðr makes no objection to being kissed; Azalaïs, how-

ever, cries out and wants the poet Peire to be put to death. Steingerðr's husband demands, and gets, legal compensation for the offence to his honour—first rings, then (after the King of Norway's mediation) also gold; Azalaïs's husband is so fond of Peire Vidal that he pleads with his wife to be reasonable and to give the stolen kiss back to the poet (who, quite unlike Kormakr, had meanwhile fled the land in terror for his life).

In the Provençal, the grotesque episodes form a pattern: each time that Uc chooses verses from a lyric of Peire's and extends them over-literally, it is for the sake of creating a particular persona, portraying a madcap poet who again and again *takes* things over-literally, who acts out a fantasy life—as emperor, as lycanthrope, as stealer of kisses, and as tongue-cut martyr of *médisance*.

There were other kinds of prosimetric narrative in the European Middle Ages, showing relations between prose and verse, and uses of verse in a prose frame, that are not exemplified in the poets' sagas I have adduced. Some such uses can be seen in the two most influential clusters of romance-matter that the Middle Ages inherited from late Antiquity—those of Alexander the Great and Apollonius of Tyre. I use the term "clusters", because in each case the transmission of the material is fraught with diversity. For both these romantic heroes—Alexander ultimately historical, Apollonius wholly fictional—we have narrative texts that are often defective, often corrupt, that exist in a range of variant versions, sometimes showing literary and scribal variations, sometimes contamination, but at other times also reflecting varying oral traditions that lie behind the extant written material.

The *Greek Alexander Romance,* often known as Pseudo-Callisthenes,[47] has verses in at least some of its versions for certain high points in the narrative, and for moments of exceptional solemnity— hymns, prophecies, prayers, epiphanies of doom. There is a hymn of praise for the young Alexander, as he returns home having won the chariot race at the Olympic Games (I 20);[48] Alexander's oracle from the god Ammon is in verse (I 30, 33), as is the dream-revelation of his destiny by the god Sarapis (I 33). The longest and most impassioned verse interlude in the romance is the plea that the flautist Ismenias makes on behalf of Thebes as Alexander is about to destroy the city. Ismenias' poetic prayer to Alexander gradually becomes an

allusive legendary history of Thebes and of all the past tragedies—
the fates of Oedipus, Semele, Heracles, Pentheus, Actaeon and many
others—which it had known (I 46a). Ismenias' meaning is, that if
Alexander destroys Thebes by fire, he will renew and culminate the
city's fatalities and at the same time destroy in himself the divine
spark to which he is heir:

μὴ θῇς ἐρήμους τούς σε σπείραντας θεούς,
τῶν σῶν γενεαρχῶν μὴ καθαιρήσῃς πόλιν.
ἰδίαν σοῦ πατρίδα μὴ ἀγνοῶν κατασκάψῃς ...
τοῦ<θ'> Ἡρακλῆος τέμενος ἦν, τὸ μὲν πρῶτον
Ἀμφιτρύωνος οἶκος· ὧδ' ἐκοιμήθη
τρεῖς νύκτας ὁ Ζεὺς εἰς μίαν ἀριθμήσας.
ὁρᾷς ἐκείνους τοὺς πεφλεγμένους οἴκους
ἀκμὴν ἔτ' ἐκστάζοντας οὐρανοῦ μῆνιν;
ἐκεῖ κεραυνῷ τὴν ποθουμένην βάλλει
Σεμέλην ποθ' ὁ Ζεύς ...

σεαυτοῦ τεμένη ἀγνοῶν θέλεις φλέξαι;
τί τοὺς γονῆας τοὺς τεκόντας ὑβρίζεις,
γένος Ἡρακλῆος <ὧν τε> καὶ κλυτοῦ Βάκχου;[49]

Do not turn the gods, that sowed you, into a desert,
do not wipe away your ancestors' city—
do not, unknowing, dash down your own fatherland ...
This was Heracles' sanctuary, formerly
Amphitryon's house: here Zeus lay,
counting three nights as one.
Do you see those houses, burnt to cinders,
from which even now the anger of heaven wells?
There, once, Zeus with a thunderbolt struck
his longed-for Semele ...

Do you mean, unknowing, to burn down your own sanctuary?
Why commit an outrage against your begetters,
child of Heracles and glorious Bacchus?

This is followed at once by a horrendous verse ecphrasis, a
description of Alexander's massacre of the Thebans, as he razes their
city to the ground. Verse is used once more, at the close of the

romance, to create a sense of awe for Alexander's dying words (III 33).[50]

Not all the verse passages in the Greek have their equivalent in the fourth-century Latin adaptation by Julius Valerius;[51] moreover, Julius' full text was rare in the medieval West, and the *Epitome* of it, which was very widely read, was entirely in prose.[52] So the experience of a popular romance of Antiquity as a prosimetric work came to the Latin Middle Ages far less by way of Alexander than of Apollonius.

The Latin *Apollonius*—itself an epitome, made towards 500 A.D., of a Greek romance, some three centuries older, that is almost wholly lost—survives in two principal and many mixed versions, in well over a hundred manuscripts[53]—yet no manuscript or version of the Latin is free from lacunae and from garbling.[54] *Apollonius* has not been much loved by classical scholars. Yet if we can look past the many defects of textual transmission, and can be tolerant of what by classical standards is "bad Latin"—the mixture of colloquialisms, Christian words, Greek words, and at times slightly hazy syntax—I think it is still possible to glimpse a moving story, candidly and sensitively told, and to realise why that story should have captured the imagination of listeners, readers and writers from late Antiquity to Shakespeare and beyond.[55]

What of the verses in *Apollonius*? Peter Parsons writes, "the Latin version which we have dates from the Christian period; and the verses are so inept that they are likely to belong to this stage".[56] The two Greek papyrus fragments that mention Apollonius are in prose, and allow no conjecture about the function of verses in the whole;[57] yet in the Latin, verses seem to me to play a vital rôle in the dramatic structure. They embody three crucial moments in the telling. The first occurs when Apollonius, hunted everywhere by the incestuous king, Antiochus, whose fateful riddle he has guessed, sailing hopelessly from port to port in order to escape him, encounters a tempest on the ocean soon after leaving Tarsus. The surviving text of the tempest verses is corrupt and incomplete. They are intense, *pathétique*, larger than life—"The sea batters the stars, the firmament" (*Pulsat mare sidera, caelum*).[58] To achieve a high style for such a

moment, the writer draws on Vergilian and Ovidian diction[59]—
though the verses are by no means a mere cento, as is sometimes
claimed. And they are not inept: they form a "hidden comparison"
(collatio occulta)[60] for the hero's inner turmoil and the despair that
threatens to engulf him. Even more, they foreshadow the later devel-
opment of the story. They are preceded in the prose by the words
(which again show a Vergilian reminiscence), "the faith of the ocean
suddenly changed" *(subito mutata est pelagi fides)*.[61] Apollonius does
not yet know the true nature of his "dearest ones" *(carissimi)*, Stran-
guillio and Dionysias, whose faith does suffer a sea-change, so that
they try to murder Tarsia, Apollonius' daughter.

The next poetic interlude is the song of that daughter, who had
escaped death only to be sold to a pander, coming to sing of her
wretched plight to her father, who does not know who she is and
believes Tarsia to be dead:

> Per sordes gradior, sed sordis conscia non sum,
> Sicut rosa in spinis nescit compungi mucrone.
> Piratae me rapuerunt, gladio ferientes iniquo,
> Lenoni nunc vendita, numquam violavi pudorem.
> Ni fletus et lucti et lacrimae de amissis inessent,
> Nulla me melior, pater si nosset ubi essem . . .[62]

> I walk through foulness, not conscious of foulness—
> as the rose among thorns cannot be pierced by thorns.
> Pirates snatched me, slashing with impious swords;
> even now, sold to a brothel-keeper, I've never spoilt my pure
>   life.
> Were it not for weeping and griefs and tears for those I've lost,
> none would be more blest than I—if my father knew where I
>   was . . .

The verses—except for the first—are unclassical in metre: they
have something of hexameters about them, but stresses, not quantities, predominate. Yet (perhaps partly because of their roughness)
they are alive, and can touch the listener as readily as they touched
Apollonius.

The final verses are the borrowed ones: a series of poetic riddles drawn from the fourth- or fifth-century collection known as *Aenigmata Symphosii*. But to say this drily does not begin to suggest how brilliant is this author's theft: his choice and ordering of riddles here, and his variations on their wording,[63] all serve to create for Tarsia a series of "hidden comparisons", by means of which—like Philosophia challenging Boethius—she rouses the despairing hero out of his lethargy. The riddles waken in Apollonius more and more reminiscences of his past and his destiny, and prepare the brutal, climactic recognition of his daughter. The effect is as of a miracle: Tarsia, who was an infant when her father last saw her, cannot know consciously "what images return"[64] in her riddles. She sets ten in all, each in three lines of verse, and her father, by solving them without fail, "shows he is truly a king". The first:

> Est domus in terris clara quae voce resultat;
> ipsa domus resonat, tacitus sed non sonat hospes;
> ambo tamen currunt, hospes simul et domus una.[65]

> There is a house on earth that echoes with clear note;
> the house itself resounds, but not its silent guest;
> and yet they both—house and guest—race together.

—where the house is a wave, and its mute guest, a fish—is one of five that evoke memories of the sea and seashore, which had played so large a part in Apollonius' calamities. The other sea-riddles reveal a reed at the water's edge, a ship, an anchor, and a sponge. Then there are two whose answers—baths[66] and ball—recall key elements in the scene that had led the shipwrecked hero to his beloved, Tarsia's mother. I would likewise see the last three riddles—whose answers are mirror, chariot, and ladder—as chosen with symbolic design: they prefigure Apollonius' recognising his true self again, re-entering the human world splendidly, and at last mounting the throne that was his due.[67]

The death-giving riddle of Antiochus' incest at the opening of the story was in prose; Tarsia's life-giving riddles are in verse. The three poetic moments—the sea-storm, within and without, the rending self-revelation of Tarsia, and the enigmas by which she prepares her sorrowing father to face life again—are used like musical motifs, orchestrated in the whole.

Besides the prosimetric narratives that reflect the variants of oral tellings, and those in which the verses existed before the prose frame, there are—though much more rarely—examples of a mixed narrative form where a single artistic imagination can be perceived shaping the verse and prose as a unity.[68] The subtlest medieval instance known to me is the Old French *Aucassin et Nicolette*, composed perhaps ca. 1200.[69] This is also one of the very few *prosimetra* I know in which the poetic passages were definitely meant for singing and not reciting: they are preserved with their music in the unique manuscript of the work. Before turning to the text, let me pause briefly with two other works in which prose narrative alternated with song.

In the immense, still largely unpublished, Old French prose *Tristan*, lyrical *lais* are interspersed, attributed to Tristan, Yseut, and other characters. These lyrical pieces, to cite Emmanuèle Baumgartner, appear "as the necessary, natural and harmonious extension of the narrative".[70] They do not exist prior to the prose. They are presented as the characters' spontaneous reactions to particular situations, in which each of them composes and performs an extended *cantilena*—their "Song to Remember". The music of seventeen of these *lais* in the *Tristan* is preserved in one of the manuscripts, of about 1300,[71] and has been edited along with the poetry.[72] The other text I would mention here is perhaps more surprising: it is Boethius' *Consolation of Philosophy,* as it was envisaged in Germany and England in the earlier eleventh century. It has long been known that, from ninth-century Limoges onwards, some of the *metra* in the *Consolatio* were set to music; it is only recently, with the rediscovery of a missing leaf from the famous manuscript that includes the "Cambridge Songs",[73] that we know of a context in which all thirty-nine poems in Boethius' work were destined for lyrical performance. At the imperial court of Henry III, where the exemplar of the song collection was probably put together in the 1040s, and at the cathedral school of Canterbury, where the extant copy was made in the following decade, a reading of the *Consolatio* will have been rendered more delightful by the singing of the poems. While it is possible that on occasion the whole work was delivered by only one performer, in general it seems likelier that there were two. As the *Consolatio* is narrated by Boethius in the first person, the narrator will probably also have sung the four poems that are put in the mouth of Boethius the character; a second performer will have spoken Philosophia's parts of the dialogue and sung the remaining thirty-five songs (including the one [II, m. 2] in which Philosophia impersonates Fortuna). A complete recital with music would have lasted some five hours, and hence might well have been spread over more than one occasion.

Aucassin et Nicolette is brief enough to be performed entire in less than two hours. The regular rubrics in the manuscript give some clues, I believe, as to the mode of performance. The passages for singing are headed "Or se cante" (Now is sung); those for speaking, "Or dient et content et fablent" (Now they speak, and narrate and converse). The first verb, *dire,* sets these passages off from the sung ones, the other two, *conter* and *fabloier,* indicate a distinction between narrated passages and dialogue.[74] The three plurals—including "they converse"—make clear that the author thought in terms of more than one performer.

The narrator sings solo in the prelude and conclusion, and in four other pieces. The function of the poetry in these is unusual among prosimetric narratives: it is to recapitulate the preceding prose as well as to advance the telling of the story.[75] The protagonists, Aucassin and Nicolette, each have one solo lyric, expressing the ardent love that they feel; the remaining sung passages are chiefly duets. The narrator shares four of these with Aucassin, and five with Nicolette, but he also has one with the *Gaite,* the loyal watchman who warns the lovers of danger, and one with the shepherd-boy who, having been well bribed, helps to reunite the lovers in the forest. Finally the songs include one trio, where the narrator frames a brief dialogue between the lovers.

These preliminary observations serve to indicate a work that is artistically ambitious in scope. Even if the narrator, who adopts a jongleur's stance, tells his tale with ostensible naïveness, and the plot engages popular motifs of folklore and carnival, as well as of romance and fairy-tale, the choice of language throughout shows a self-conscious maker's fastidiousness. It is clear that the anonymous author—he, or possibly she—is cultivated and has received the education of the learned, clerical world. This can be seen even in a small, impish detail in one of the most celebrated passages, where Aucassin declares he would rather go to hell—of course, with Nicolette—than enter paradise. His knowingly perverse evocations both of paradise and hell start, revealingly, with the clergy: into paradise go "the old priests and the old cripples and the one-armed folk who huddle before the altars and in the old crypts day and night"—in a word, the decrepit and the wretched; into hell go "the fine clerks and the fine knights . . . the fair courtly ladies who have two lovers, or three, besides their husband . . . harpers and minstrels and the kings of the world".[76] The irony that lurks here betrays a clerically formed imagination.

Aucassin et Nicolette is indeed profoundly Menippean in spirit: the purpose of this love-story, in nearly all its facets, is the witty and disconcerting testing of truth. The truth of the ideas of the *bienpensants* is undermined over and over again. The official meaning of hell and paradise is called in question—but so is that of chivalric honour. If love is thought to spur a man to knightly deeds, it does the opposite to Aucassin: his chivalric aspirations mean nothing to him when his father, Count Garin, will not let him marry Nicolette. In the Count's eyes, she is nothing but a Saracen slave-girl. It is in the land of Torelore (we might translate, the land of Nonny-no)—the region where all *bienpensant* expectations are reversed—that Nicolette is at once perceived as nobly born and desired as a princess. Aucassin belongs sufficiently to his father's world to behave brutishly in Torelore: as the King there mimes a *couvade*, feigning to be recovering from giving birth,[77] Aucassin beats the King nearly to death, and addresses him with unexpected coarseness: "Wicked son of a bitch!" *(Malvais fix a putain!).*[78] During the mock-battle in Torelore, where the knights, led by the Queen, fight with rotten apples, eggs and *fromage frais,* Aucassin fights in earnest, "killing many people". We know of such comic combats, waged with food, from medieval carnival celebrations (a notable literary transformation is the battle between Don Carnal and Quaresma—Lady Lent—in the *Libro de Buen Amor*);[79] but Aucassin harshly breaks the carnival spirit.

The Arcadian world that seems to lie at the edges of the story cannot, within the narrative, banish the spectre of cruelty—neither here nor earlier, in the repeated threats that Nicolette will be burnt alive (for no other reason than that she exists and that Aucassin insists on marrying her). The seemingly bland introduction of cruelty is a frequent feature of Menippean works from Petronius and Seneca onwards: "They do but jest, poison in jest." At the same time, the author of *Aucassin et Nicolette* is sensitively aware of the converse: the King of Torelore, contemptible in Aucassin's eyes because of his womanly mime, has a lesson for the young chevalier: "Sir, you have gone too far: it is not our custom to kill one another."[80]

The author has other, equally perceptive ways of testing what is real and what is serious—as for instance when he juxtaposes Aucassin torn by brambles as he rides in search of Nicolette, "bleeding in forty places—or at least in thirty", and the oxherd whom Aucassin meets, hungry and afraid, so poor that his mother had her mattress taken away from her and slept on straw.[81]

I should like to focus more closely on at least one motif in the work. Nicolette, to enable Aucassin to find her in the forest, leaves a message for him with the shepherd-boys whom she finds breakfasting at the forest's edge. Her message is a riddle, that in its function is like Tarsia's life-giving riddles in the *Apollonius*: it can confer bliss on him who solves it:

> Se Dix vos aït, bel enfant, fait ele, dites li qu'il a une beste en ceste forest et qu'i le viegne cacier, et s'il l'i puet prendre, il n'en donroit mie un menbre por cent mars d'or, non por cinc cens, ne por nul avoir . . .
> Le beste a tel mecine que Aucassins ert garis de son mehaing; et j'ai ci cinc sous en me borse: tenés, se li dites; et dedens trois jors li covient cacier, et se il dens trois jors ne le trove, ja mais n'iert garis de son mehaig.[82]

> Dear children, she said, in God's name tell him there is a beast in this forest and that he should come to hunt it,[83] and if he can catch it, he wouldn't give up even one of its limbs for a hundred gold marks, not for five hundred, nor for all the wealth there is . . .
> The beast has a healing power that will cure Aucassin of his wound; and I've got five sous here in my purse—take them and tell him! And he must hunt within three days, and if in three days he doesn't find the beast, he'll never be cured of his wound.

The Ovidian and medieval courtly theme of the love-malady, to which Nicolette alludes—the lover, sick and wounded, can be healed only by the beloved[84]—had been prefigured in an earlier, lyrical passage, where Aucassin sings:

L'autr'ier vi un pelerin,
nés estoit de Limosin,
malades de l'esvertin
si gisoit ens en un lit:
mout par estoit entrepris,
de grant mal amaladis.
Tu passas devant son lit,
si soulevas ton traïn
et ton peliçon ermin,
la cemisse de blanc lin,
tant que ta ganbete vit:
garis fu li pelerins
et tos sains, ainc ne fu si.[85]

The other day I saw a pilgrim,
a native of the Limousin,
afflicted by madness,
lying in a bed
in a very sorry state,
sick with grievous malady.
You passed before his bed,
you lifted up your train,
your ermine cape
and your white linen shift,
so far that he saw your pretty leg:
the pilgrim was cured—
never had he been so well.

The verse and prose together, by their diverse uses of wit, probe the erotic topos of the beloved as miraculous healer, in all its ambiguities. Through Aucassin's eyes we see Nicolette's uncourtly gesture and its amazing effect. Like the heroines of Greek romances—Chloe, Anthia, Chrysorrhoe and the rest—Nicolette has an open, innocent sensuality which she never conceals from Aucassin. The poet leaves it for the listener to decide whether Nicolette's was a casual gesture, unrelated to the pilgrim, or was a gesture of numinous healing. By strategically associating the medical imagery with the two very different moments, he prompts the listener to think back—once he has comprehended Nicolette's riddle—and to wonder, was it a therapeutic *love* that she'd inspired in the pilgrim too? Yet he lets no such suspicion enter Aucassin's thought. He enables his audience to perceive both what is comic and what is precious about the love of his hero and heroine.

The full imaginative resonance of Nicolette's healing Aucassin, however, depends not only on recalling the pilgrim but on knowing and recalling how Philosophia healed Boethius. From the time the lovers find each other in the forest to their complete union at the close of the tale, Nicolette plays the rôle of Philosophia in relation to Aucassin. Alone he is hopeless, while she is shown as having all the understanding that he lacks; it is she who takes the unfailing initiative during all their misadventures, and who at last leads her impulsive, grief-stricken devotee to a felicity he could never have attained without her help.

The misadventures prior to that felicity belong for the most part to the *koinê* of Greek romance. There are, as in *Apollonius* and in the late-antique and Byzantine Greek examples, the storms at sea that decide the destiny of the protagonists—either pulling them apart or half-miraculously reuniting them. There are the shipwrecks, there is the heroine's abduction, her recognition by her royal father, and the sexual threats to which she is exposed. The conjunction of these motifs with the more unusual one of the life-giving riddle makes me suspect that the Old French author held the story of Apollonius particularly dear. Other aspects of his *conjointure*—such as the kingdom of Torelore—stem from a rather different, popular carnival tradition.[86] Yet playing over all the motifs in *Aucassin et Nicolette*, and transforming them, is a truth-testing, searchingly Menippean, Boethian imagination.

Boethius the character was consoled and healed by Philosophia; Boethius the author has left us a work that can console and heal those who hear or read it. What Philosophia does for Boethius, the text can do for us. This parallel, left unstated in the *Consolatio*, is played upon and rendered explicit by the author of *Aucassin et Nico-*

lette. As Nicolette could heal both her beloved and the pilgrim, even so—the author assures his audience at the outset—can his composition heal:

> Nus hom n'est si esbahis,
> tant dolans ni entrepris,
> de grant mal amaladis,
> se il l'oit, ne soit garis
> et de joie resbaudis,
>   tant par est douce.[87]

> There is no man so downcast,
> sorrowing or in sorry state,
> so sick with grievous malady
> that, if he hears it, is not healed,
> strengthened once again by joy—
>   so great is its gentleness.

IV

The Poetic and the Empirical "I"

In this concluding chapter I should like to look in more detail, by way of five examples, at what happens when an author using the mixed form is a first-person protagonist in his or her work. We have already seen some instances of this, notably with Boethius and Hildebert; but the device also extends to some highly individual structures of other kinds than theirs. The first two on which I wish to make some observations belong to the early Middle Ages: Dhuoda's *Liber manualis* (841–3), and Rather of Verona's *Phrenesis* (955). After that I shall try to suggest some comparisons between three masterpieces of the later thirteenth century that narrate and analyse diverse experiences of love: Mechthild of Magdeburg's *Fliessendes Licht der Gottheit* (ca. 1250–83), Marguerite Porete's *Mirouer des simples ames* (ca. 1285–95), and Dante's *Vita Nuova* (1293–4).

To two of these works—those of Dhuoda and Marguerite Porete—I devoted chapters in a book I wrote a decade ago, called *Women Writers of the Middle Ages.*[1] There my concern was especially with the individuality of thought and expression in Dhuoda's and Marguerite's writing, and with the ways in which these two women understood themselves. I had not yet seen the significance of their choice of the mixed form, nor seen how and why that choice was propitious for the presentation of shifting perspectives, the use of diverse authorial voices, in the two works. That is why I should like to return to these two *prosimetra* briefly among my illustrations.

It may be useful, to begin with, to recall a distinction made by Leo Spitzer,[2] between the *empirical "I"* of a poet—that is, the specific personality revealed in the writing—and the *poetic "I"*, which can stand for "the human soul as such",[3] and which enables an author to speak representatively, on behalf of humanity. It is possible that, as Spitzer argues, "in the Middle Ages, the 'poetic I' had more freedom and more breadth than it has today". I am not happy, however, when Spitzer goes on to claim that, if the medieval public saw the poetic "I" as representative of humanity, "we must assume that . . . it was interested only in this representative rôle of the poet . . . It was a trifling matter who the empirical person behind this 'I' actually was."[4] On the contrary, I would suggest it was the well-matched interplay of the poetic with the empirical, the universalising with the specific, the exemplary-didactic with the uniquely-perceiving, that characterised some of the most exciting literary achievements, and that proved to be particularly congenial to the mixed form.

To comprehend the empirical "I" of Dhuoda, we must recall at least swiftly the circumstances in which her book was composed. These she reveals in the course of her book[5]—there is little external evidence about her in surviving historical sources. In 824 this Frankish, or perhaps Catalan, noblewoman married Bernard, Duke of Septimania, one of the leading contenders for power in the dangerous, strife-torn world of Charlemagne's heirs. By him she had a son, William; then Bernard dispatched her to southern France, abandoning her totally save for one brief visit, sixteen years later, during which she conceived a second son. In 841 Bernard sent William as a hostage to the court of Charles the Bald, and had the newborn son, still unbaptised, snatched away from his mother. It was in this time of desolation that Dhuoda wrote her *Liber*. She sent it to William in 843. From sources outside the book we know that the next year Bernard was executed for treason, and William captured and executed four years later—he was aged twenty-one. In the race for sovereignty, they had fought on the losing side. About the younger son (another Bernard) nothing is known.

In the *Liber* that Dhuoda sent her son William we can perceive both a representative, poetic "I", who sets up for him ideals comparable to those in a "mirror for princes", and an empirical "I"—the mother left in solitude, the wife neglected by her husband, yet still miraculously filled with generosity of spirit and tenderness. Dhuoda probably knew the two main earlier Carolingian princes' mirrors, Smaragdus' *Via regia* and Jonas of Orléans's *De institutione regia*.[6] Some fifteen years after her own *Liber manualis*, a highly literate poet, Sedulius Scottus, was to write such a mirror using the prosimetric form, and vying with Boethius in the range and virtuosity of his verses in rare classical metres. Yet Sedulius' polished *De rectoribus Christianis*[7] is abstract and lifeless compared with Dhuoda's work. Moreover, while the ideas and values of the three clerical authors of mirrors are predictably similar, those of Dhuoda are in essential ways independent: never unchristian, but often unclerical—her piety left room for so much that was secular and humane. Her Latin, unlike that of the erudite clerics, so often shows unclassical, do-it-yourself features that its syntax, usage and prosody still set many problems. But its distinctive, enticing beauty is bound up with its revealing an empirical "I" as well as a poetic one. What Dhuoda gave her son was not simply moral-political advice: it was loving advice. To some extent we could even say that her advice itself *is* the self-portrait of a loving nature; and to that extent the poetic and the empirical "I" coincide.

While the empirical "I" throughout stresses her frailty, helplessness and lack of learning, the poetic "I" makes claims that include a conscious affirmation of form as well as content in her work:

A capite huius libelli usque ad finem, et in arte et in sensu, et metris melodie et in articulatione atque motibus fluxuum membrorum, omnia et per omnia et in omnibus ad salutem anime et corporis tui cuncta tibi scriptitata cognosce.[8]

From the beginning of this little book to its end, in its artistry and its meaning, in the measures of its lyrical parts and in the articulation and movements of the flow of clauses, recognise that everything has been written for the wellbeing of your soul and body—all these things and through all and in all.

Omnia et per omnia et in omnibus: it is as if Dhuoda saw the Trinity—the Father embracing all, the Logos through whom all is made, the Spirit dwelling in all—pervading her writing. Form and content, verse and prose, are, she claims, equally dedicated to William's *salus:* each can show him a principle of order—melodic measure and prose articulation—that may attract him by its art and persuade him by its sense. The unity of the two kinds of order in the writing is symbolic of that between writer and reader, mother and son. Thus Dhuoda goes on to ask of William the same devoted attentiveness as recipient that she has given her book as begetter: "When the work has been sent to you by my hand, I want you to embrace it joyfully with yours, and holding it, turning and reading it, strive to accomplish it most excellently."[9]

The prose then evokes the empirical situation—Dhuoda bereft of both her beloved children, William's great distance from her—and how the book will render the absent mother present to her son. It is a mirror in which he will see her face as well as his own. But the long verse prologue that follows (the *Epigrama,* as Dhuoda calls it) begins as it were far more objectively. Solemnly she invokes God, commending William to him. In her prayer to God, however, Dhuoda is at the same time addressing William, outlining her ideals for him, ideals that are this-worldly as much as other-worldly:

> Iubilet iocundus   cursu felici,
> Pergat cum virtute   fulgens ad supra . . .
>
> Veniat in eum   larga tua gratia,
> Pax et securitas   corporis et mente,
>
> In quo in seculo   vigeat cum prole,
> Ita tenens ista   careat ne illa.[10]

May he jubilate joyously, through a glad course of life,
radiant in virtue, may he reach the heights . . .

May your generous grace penetrate him,
with peace and security of body and mind,

In which he may flourish in the world, and have children,
holding what's here so as not to lose what's there.

A few lines later the empirical "I", unique in its claim on the son she loves, emerges in the language of the *orante:*

Mis michi similem   non habebit unquam,
Quanquam indignam[11]   genitrixque sua.

The archaic genitive *mis,* which Dhuoda had learnt from Donatus, is added to *michi* to give unusual emphasis:

He'll never have anyone like me, like me—
I who, though unworthy, am also his mother.

The prayer to God closes with Dhuoda's plea for both her children: "Let them live, I beseech you, and may they love you always." But the poem, of forty couplets, is not yet complete: in four others, Dhuoda explains the acrostic in what had gone before, the initial letters that set in relief the specificity of her prayer. Overtly she had not named herself, yet in the acrostic she had done so. If the prayer became known outside its immediate context, a discerning reader would realise who this mother had been. That Dhuoda was addressing not only God and William, but potentially also a wider world, becomes clear in these final couplets, which begin with the word *Lector* and add the acrostic *Lege,* in which Dhuoda begs her future reader to pray for her reunion with husband and children in heaven.

The prose prologue that follows these verses[12] develops the mirror-image that had appeared fugitively in the earlier sentences. Dhuoda now evokes a courtly world, of young men playing at dice and young women verifying their beauty in mirrors, to suggest that her *speculum* for William, in which he can verify his inner beauty, is not meant as a sermon but as a delight: "use it as if it were a matter of mirrors or of games at dice". Here the more representative, didactic rôle is subsumed in the more specific personal one: the instructress reveals herself an enchanting companion.

In the main body of the *Liber* verse plays a relatively minor part.[13] Dhuoda adduces verses by "a certain poet", "a certain teacher" (*quidam poeta, quidam doctor*), and now and then just by "someone" (*quidam*).[14] At times she is adapting a known poet, such as Prudentius, at others the verses are probably her own, though, in order to give herself an appropriate *auctoritas,* she doesn't admit this—I suspect because she enjoyed at least a touch of that ludic mystification which "Aethicus Ister" had used so riotously.[15]

There is a larger group of verses, which Dhuoda claims explicitly as hers *(ipsa dictavi),*[16] near the close of the book. They begin after a section[17] that moves from the mystic calculation of perfect numbers into a litany of blessings which Dhuoda invokes for her son. The first poem, *De temporibus tuis* (On the ages of your life), continues the play with numbers, but through this the urgent individual voice breaks out. Dhuoda warns that she is sick and near death, she cannot write a longer work for William, nor even a little one for his infant brother—so let them share these hasty notes, drinking them like mead.

There follows a longer poem in rhythmic pseudo–Sapphic stanzas. As with the couplets cited earlier, the measure is determined not by Latin quantities, and only partially by Latin stresses—it is the accentual pattern of Germanic verse, with two main stresses and a variable number of weak syllables in each half-line, that tends to predominate.[18] The strophes, like the couplets at the opening, are individuated by their acrostic. While in principle the poem is representative, telling what any mother of noble spirit might wish her son to be, it is only *this* mother who writes (as the acrostic shows) *Versi ad Vuilhelmum.* The strophes are also individuated by their subtle transitions between the poetic "I", exhorting, and praying to God that the exhortations may come true, and the empirical "I", the mother asking herself if in God's eyes she really merits the joy of meeting her cherished son again. The moment of searching anguish comes between two strophes of a wholly different kind:[19]

> Licet iuventus tua   florida virgis
> —Quadrans quaternis   computaris in annis—
> Senioribus teneris   membris gra*datim*
>   Cursu peragrans,[20]

> Multum a me videtur   longior esse,
> Cernere volens tue   speciei tenorem—[21]
> Si daretur virtus!   et tamen ad hec merita
>   Non mea vigent.

Utinam illi vivas   qui te plasmavit,
Placida mente . . .

Though the branches of your youth are flowering
(your years now reckoned at four times four),
step by step with your tender limbs moving
          in the ranks of the lords,

It all seems much too far away from me,
I who long to see again how you look—
if only the strength were given!—and yet I'm
          not up to deserving it.

As long as you live for him who has fashioned you,
serene in your mind . . .

There is a similar oscillation in the prose that follows, where, notwithstanding repeated declarations that her book is now ended, Dhuoda passes from advice for William's public life to thoughts of her own frailty, unembittered reminiscences of the husband who had deserted her, reflections on the incomparable bond she still feels with William *(nullum similem tui)*[22]—to composing a verse epitaph that he shall set upon her tomb. From every personal reflection the empirical Dhuoda reverts to the poetic "I" of the *orante*. It is not as though the one "I" belonged to the prose, the other to the verse. The shifts occur within both verse and prose, allowing more complex interplays. But I think the flexibility of the alternating form made easy and natural the alternations of perspective.

We have only a brief and very fragmentary *prosimetrum* by Rather of Verona, the most brilliant as well as the quirkiest writer of Latin prose in the tenth century. He chose for it the fighting title *Phrenesis* (Frenzy),[23] because his enemies had claimed he was a raving lunatic *(phreneticus)*. The work was written at Mainz in 955: it was not till he was in his sixties that Rather, born ca. 890 into a noble Liégois family, produced a spate of autobiographical works, justifying himself, ironically berating himself, and most of all excoriating his fellow-men—works of which, some polemical letters apart, *Phrenesis* was the earliest.

Rather had never been popular. Difficult personally as well as stylistically, and politically inept among the mighty prelates and secular rulers of the Ottonian world, he had already twice been appointed Bishop of Verona and been twice deposed, imprisoned, and then chased out.[24] Meanwhile, through the good offices of Otto the Great and his brother, Chancellor Bruno, who had been Rather's literary disciple, Rather was given the consolation-prize of the bishopric of his native Liège. But within fifteen months an intrigue, mounted chiefly by Robert, Archbishop of Trier (an uncle of Otto's) and Baldric, Bishop of Utrecht, resulted in Rather's expulsion and in the appointment in his place of a younger Baldric, nephew of the bishop of that name. It was a humiliation that Rather was determined to combat, at least with his pen, in *Phrenesis.*

Here too we can distinguish between a poetic "I", a representative voice invoking biblical authority to denounce injustice and nepotism, and an empirical "I"—the aggrieved eccentric, caustic but ultimately helpless in the game of power. Even if we suspect that the one "I" and the other aren't humanly distinct—that is, that Rather was spurred to his crusade against the corrupt mighty ones largely by self-interest—the interplay between the two selves results in a sparkling piece of writing. The whole was a collection of pamphlets *(libelli),* only a few of which survive[25]—yet Rather also saw himself as continuing the prosimetric tradition of "Martianus, Fulgentius and Boethius".[26]

The prose *Proemium* contains the first of that inimitable series of self-portraits of Rather's, sardonic in tone and hermetic in style, self-mocking, self-concealing and self-revealing, which have been rediscovered and illuminated in our century by Georg Misch and Erich Auerbach.[27] Rather here writes of himself mainly in the third person, which gives his occasional shifts to the first a peculiar force. When, banished from Liège, a refugee in Mainz, he was taunted as a lunatic by his opponents for trying to set down what had been done to him, "At that insult he embraced again the ardour of writing, rekindled now though it had been lulled before . . . calling himself a madman in accordance with their view—since, in a way that is quite exceptional today, in such a crisis he takes refuge not in bribery or in armed combat, as some do, nor in a multitude of friends, but in books, library-shelves, the judgements of the ancients."[28] Rather proceeds to demonstrate his "madness" by deliberate mystification of his paradoxical character: thus for instance:

> irasci visus fuit sepe letissimus, letus item maximum intus celavit sepe dolorem. Dabat non rogatus, impatiens rogari, ignotum sepius odium quasi retinens lesus, multaque in hunc actitaverat deprehendi perdifficilis modum.[29]

> often he seemed angry and yet was completely happy, often he seemed happy yet concealed a deep sorrow within. He gave without being asked—as he couldn't bear being asked. When hurt, he often as it were held back his hatred, not letting it be known—that was his way in many of his concerns: he was very difficult to comprehend.

Rather's mystification of style is equally deliberate—is indeed another aspect of his character. He alludes to the tortuousness of his prose, to its "very frequent use of parenthesis", and at the same time he uses it as a challenge, boasting: "Whoever complains that he lacks the capacity to understand such writing as this, it's idle for him to pretend to Latinity" *(frustra etiam sibi arrogat Latinitatem, ad talia qui capienda deesse sibi conqueritur facultatem).*[30]

In the prosimetric diatribe that follows this *Proemium*, Rather is addressing his chief enemy, Robert of Trier. Almost at once he mentions a rumour that Robert had died—a false rumour, but "with perhaps no absolutely vain omen".[31] I shall return to this rumour soon—even as Rather returns to it several times. But first I would pause with at least one memorable moment in the vehement self-justification and polemic, which shows the oscillation between the poetic and the empirical "I". The empirical Rather again proudly asserts his lunacy: he, a deposed bishop, had dared publicly to "excommunicate" the mighty Archbishop Robert, who had come to Liège for the Easter days of 955, to keep order after the deposition: Rather had declared the archbishop unfit to take communion, citing words from the Sermon on the Mount (Matthew 5, 23–24) in support of his claim:

cum in Cenae Domini festo ... muliercularum, moris ut est, reciperetis oblata, istud inferri vobis phrenetica eius pariter fecit audacia ..."Si offers munus tuum ad altare et ibi recordatus fueris, quia frater tuus habet aliquid adversum te, relinque ibi munus tuum ante altare, et vade prius reconciliari fratri tuo ..."

when, on Maundy Thursday ... you received the women's offerings, as is the custom, the phrenetic audacity of that Rather had these words brought before you as well ..."If you offer your gift at the altar, and there remember that your brother has something against you, leave your offering before the altar and go and be reconciled with your brother first ..."

Was it in truth a "phrenetic audacity" of Rather's thus publicly to outface his superior in the hierarchy? Or did that *phrenesis* perhaps lie in the archbishop's taking communion with such a wrong on his conscience? Switching suddenly to the first person, Rather pounces:

Hic, domine, ambigo, cuiusvis duorum mirari debeam amplius phrenesim.[32]

Here, my lord, I wonder whose frenzy—yours or mine—I ought to marvel at more.

Towards the close, Rather returns to the rumour of Robert's death, this time with histrionic pathos: "Ah be silent, silent, I beg you, silent, for now the message is that my enemy is no more!"[33] Is this message any more to be trusted than the earlier ones? I see no reason to suppose so. First, it is followed by a series of deft allusions to the satirists—Persius, Juvenal, Horace—in the midst of which Rather slips in his own phrase, "it's useless to pursue plebeian gossip".[34] Second, because Rather had left Mainz, where he composed *Phrenesis* and unleashed it on the world, for a monastery in Belgium before the end of 955, and Robert did not in fact die till May 19, 956. Did he lie dying for so many months, or were the rumours perhaps Rather's own invention? At all events, the wording of the elegy in memory of Robert, that soon follows, strongly suggests to me that it was written to needle a man whom Rather still had good reason to suppose alive.

The elegy is preceded by seventy dark hexameters, which the first editors gave up as incomprehensible[35] and which have not been explained since. Rather denounces the injustices he has suffered, with the help of Old Testament *figurae:* he is the confounded "Nathan of the Lord"; he sees fulfilled in his own ordeal in the Church the internecine strife that Isaiah (9, 20) had prophesied:

> Sic ruit in preceps decus et veneratio prorsus
> Ordinibus collata sacris et celitus, ac sic
> Ephraim Manassen, Manasses infestat Ephraim,
> Debellare simul Iudam tenduntque parati . . .[36]

> Thus honour and the reverence heaven brings
> to holy orders tumbles headlong, thus Ephraim
> attacks Manasses and Manasses Ephraim,
> and together they set out to destroy Judah . . .

But Rather ends with the prophetic "I" giving way to the petulant empirical one, cursing the "perfidious phalanx" of his enemies and determined to reclaim all that he believed was rightfully his:

> . . . vincet nam mox Deus ipse,
> Vincet et ipsa suo victrix Constantia recto
> Semper, et haec comitata suis fautricibus omnes
> Infestos, nocuos, inimicos proterat hostes,
> Vincat, perturbet, mutilet, rogo, postulo, posco—
> "Amen, sic fiat" reboent, et cuncta reposco![37]

> . . . soon God himself shall win,
> and Constancy, her right hand ever victorious,
> shall win, escorted by all those who favour her,
> shall crush the loathsome, harmful, hostile foes,
> beat, ravage, mutilate them, as I ask, beseech, demand—
> let them echo "Amen", and I'll demand back all!

The elegiac couplets for Robert that follow seem to begin harmlessly—"Spare your servant, oh God"—but soon reveal themselves as barbed. Rather's prayer for his enemy continues: "he is known to have sinned—nothing against me, for I am nothing in your sight—

but he was one who tried to sacrifice another's flock". Overtly, Rather is praying that Robert may "walk the starry ways of heaven"; yet he couches this, uniquely, in a series of negatives, in which it sounds as though Robert had been relegated to a pagan underworld. From "Let him blithely disdain Charon" (*Porthmea*[38] *contempnat felix*) Rather passes to the imprecations:

> Nec lamas Erebi tangat nigrasque paludes,
>   Cerberus absistat, Gorgona despiciat,
> Nec Stygios innare lacus aut tetra videre
>   Tartara contingat, quem via dextra iuvat,
> Nec Chaos aut Phlegethon nigris habitacula monstris
>   Sint, que vel subeat vel subeunda fleat.[39]

> Let him not touch the mire of Erebus or its black marshes,
> let Cerberus hold back, let him shun the Gorgon's face,
> let him not have to swim the Stygian lakes or see
> foul Tartarus, this man whom the right path guides;
> let Chaos and Phlegethon, the dwellings of black monsters,
> not be the places where he sinks or, sinking, weeps!

In the final couplet the "miching mallecho, that means mischief" is palpable:

> Sic mea te vexat, sic, o Rodberte, *Phrenesis,*
>   Sic, inquam, felix sis, rogat, ac fueris.

> As much, Robert, as much as my *Phrenesis* annoys you,
> so much, I say, does it pray for your happiness, now and in future.

This seems to me the clearest indication that the "elegy" was—deliberately—premature.[40]

Why did Rather in *Phrenesis*, for the only time in his surviving works, have recourse to poetry as well as prose? I think the brief answer is "poetic licence": in these poems, Rather could allow himself certain kinds of audacity that would scarcely have been possible in prose. In the stylised forms he could most readily conjoin prophecy and spitefulness, dirge and grudge, a poetic and an empirical "I".

There is no historical link between Dhuoda's and Rather's experiments with *prosimetra* in the ninth and tenth centuries and the unusual vernacular works of the late thirteenth with which I should like to conclude. Yet it seems to me that any consideration of the art and scope of the mixed form, from Antiquity to the Middle Ages—even the most selective—would be seriously wanting if it did not at least signal, and reflect upon some aspects of, the art and scope of these later achievements.

To begin with some simple comparisons. Mechthild's *Fliessendes Licht*, Marguerite's *Mirouer* and Dante's *Vita Nuova*[41] all include a substantial amount of lyrical love-poetry in the midst of their prose. All three works are concerned not only with the Christian God but with a divine personification called Love, who in each work converses with the first-person narrator, or with the soul of that empirical "I". In medieval German and medieval French, where the word for Love is grammatically feminine *(Minne, Amour),* this personified Love is conceived as a divine womanly being—Mechthild's partner Minne, Marguerite's Amour.[42] In Italian, however, *Amore* is grammatically masculine, and the figure who appears to Dante in his dreams is "a lord of fearsome aspect", or again "a young man clothed in the whitest robes" (an expression reminiscent of biblical evocations of angels).[43]

All three writers depict the sensation of love with keen stringency, as an overmastering, suprahuman force. The emotions depicted range from sublime raptures to desperate sorrows. Moreover, while all three portray these raptures and sorrows as moments lived by an empirical "I", they show themselves equally aware of a poetic "I", of a rôle in which all that is undergone becomes exemplary.

All three, finally, include a significant proportion of elements which might seem, to a romantic (or post-Romantic) reader, to be quite incompatible with the evocation of ardent inner experiences. These elements are analytic, seemingly pedantic—dividing, enumerating and articulating the sublimities and the griefs. Thus for instance, among the sections of Mechthild's first Book, God curses the narrator in eight ways (7), the lowliest being praises God in ten ways (8), God offers four, and then again five, comparisons for the soul (16, 18), and caresses the soul in six ways (19), while the soul in answer praises God first in five ways (17) and then in six (20). Similarly in Marguerite's *Mirouer:* knowledge of the soul is revealed by Amour in nine points (11), Amour enumerates three deaths (60) and seven states of the soul (61), and the narrator, ten ways of looking (*regars*—123–130). In the *Vita Nuova,* the structure of nearly every sonnet, the ballata and each canzone, is explained by way of a series of divisions and even—in the canzoni—subdivisions. I shall discuss the reasons for the presence of such "divisive" elements in all three works a little later. For the present, I would set alongside the points of resemblance among the three certain points of contrast.

Often the poetry and prose in the writing of Mechthild and Marguerite are not clearly demarcated from each other. The poetry grows out of the prose and grows back into it. Prose sentences spill over into lyrical passages (just as the love evoked has a quality that is *débordante*); often too, if the prose itself is charged with lyricism, it changes gradually, rather than instantly, into a more regular pattern; the return journey, into irregularity, is just as easily and unselfconsciously made. While there are a few passages in the *Fliessendes Licht* and the *Mirouer* that any sensible editor would print as poetry, with many others the question remains legitimately open to editorial discretion. All this is wholly different in the *Vita Nuova,* which does not have such openness of form: poetry and prose are kept rigorously distinct at every stage. At the same time, the poetry often re-presents what has already been told in the prose: in this, Dante's technique comes close not to the women writers but to the author of *Aucassin et Nicolette.*[44]

The contrast which might spring to mind most readily to readers familiar with the two mystical works as well as the *Vita Nuova* is one between the narrator's love for God, in Mechthild and Marguerite, and Dante's love for a young woman, Beatrice. Yet that contrast, I would suggest, is not nearly as simple to sustain in detail as might at first appear. To state this succinctly is to state it with disappointing baldness: what counts is to see the *ways* in which Mechthild and Marguerite show themselves aware of an erotic dimension and Dante of a spiritual one.

Finally, there are differences of structure. Though each of the three works is far-reachingly lyrical, and each has likewise a certain narrative-dramatic element, this element is weakest in Mechthild, strongest in Dante. Neither Mechthild nor Marguerite deploys a linear structure: they return to themes over and over, in variations, different images, different modes—lyric, dialogue, allegory, mystical parable or *Märchen*. One could indeed say that their works have no overarching structure, however splendidly certain sections or episodes may be built. In the *Vita Nuova,* Dante's structure is not always easy to perceive, and the narrative thread is at times abandoned; yet unlike the works of the two women, the *Vita Nuova* moves towards a close that is a decisive close and a culmination.

It is scarcely possible, in the remainder of this chapter, to conjure up the imaginative complexity of three works of such stature, two of which, moreover, have attracted a large amount of critical study, including some of the highest distinction (I think particularly of Wolfgang Mohr on Mechthild[45] and Domenico De Robertis on the *Vita Nuova*).[46] Yet I hope that considering the two women's works and Dante's side by side for the first time may also throw certain features newly into relief.

Mechthild wrote her *Fliessendes Licht*[47] in the course of more than three decades. It consists, to cite Wolfgang Mohr, of "fragments of an inner biography".[48] These changed their manner and nature over the years. The first three of her seven "Books" are most copious in lyrical utterances and dialogues, and I shall illustrate chiefly from these. At the outset, and occasionally later, Mechthild defines and defends herself as a prophet: while her work tells "only of me", she is sending it to the whole clerical world, to people both good and evil. They must read it nine times, for its author is not the empirical "I", Mechthild, but God.[49]

The *Fliessendes Licht* is far richer in imagery than either the *Mirouer* or the *Vita Nuova*. The simplest structures in Mechthild's imagery are anaphoric. Thus, when "The lowliest being praises God in ten ways" (I 8), it is in a series of exclamations parallel in form:

> O du brennender berg,
> o du userwelte sunne,
> o du voller mane,
> o du grundeloser brunne,

o du unreichaftú höhi,
o du klarheit ane masse,
o wisheit ane grunt,
o barmherzekeit ane hinderunge,
o sterki ane widersatzunge,
o crone aller eren![50]

Oh you burning mountain,
oh you chosen sun,
oh you full moon,
oh you bottomless fountain,
oh you unattainable height,
oh you clarity without measure,
oh wisdom without ground,
oh mercy without hindrance,
oh strength without resistance,
oh crown of every honour!

The expressions range from the heights to the depths, but also from concrete to abstract. At times Mechthild takes playful delight in conjoining images and allegorical concepts incongruously, as in a prose passage (I 46) where she seizes on a moment in the Apocalypse (12, 1) for her point of departure:

Die brut ist gekleidet mit der sunnen und hat den manen under die füsse getretten, und si ist gekrönet mit der einunge. Si hat ein cappellan, das ist die vorhte. Der hat eine guldine ruote in der hant, das ist die wisheit. Der cappellan ist gekleidet mit des lambes bluot und ist mit der ere gekrönet, und dú wisheit ist gekleidet mit der wolsamikeit und ist gekrönet mit der ewekeit.

The bride is clothed with the sun and has trodden the moon beneath her feet, and she is crowned with union. She has a chaplain: that is Fear. He has a golden switch in his hand: that is Wisdom. He is clothed in the blood of the Lamb and crowned with honour, and Wisdom is clothed in delight and crowned with eternity.

Similarly, among the bridesmaids, Remorse "is clothed in little grapes and crowned with joy", Mercy "is clothed in scented oil and crowned with ecstasy".

Such transitions between physical and spiritual are used to particularly arresting effect in Mechthild's evocation of Mary at the cross (I 22), where she gives Mary the words:

"... ich sögete die propheten und die wissagen, e denne ich geborn wart. Dar nach in miner kintheit sögete ich Jhesum; fúrbas in miner jugent sögete ich gottes brut, die heligen cristanheit, bi dem crútze, da ich also dúrre und jemerlich wart, do das swert der vleischlicher pine Jhesu sneit geistlich in min sele."

> Do stuonden offen beide sine wunden und ir brúste;
> die wunden gussen, die brúste vlussen,
> also das lebendig wart die sele und gar gesunt,
> do er den blanken roten win gos in iren roten munt.

"... I gave suck to the prophets and sibyls before I was born. Then in my childhood I gave suck to Jesus; then in my youth I gave suck to God's bride, holy Christendom, at the cross, where I became so parched and pitiable, where the sword of Jesus' bodily pain cut spiritually into my soul."

> There stood open both his wounds and her breasts;
> the wounds poured, the breasts flowed,
> so that the soul became alive and healthy too,
> as he poured the bright red wine into her red mouth.

Mary is both the lamenting mother and an omnitemporal figure, an Ecclesia-like nurturer of every age; her soul in its sorrow drinks Christ's blood, and at the same time is transfused into the soul of her nursling, who drinks both Mary's milk and the blood that is the wine of the eucharist. The complementary images of drinking are characteristic of medieval women's spiritual writing. As Caroline Walker Bynum has perceptively observed, "women chose certain symbols—especially eating and pain—more frequently than did men. And the medieval notion of the female as body and food seems to have suggested that the realities of suffering and service ... somehow pressed more heavily on women"; in communion, however, a woman "became not nurturer or feeder of others but receiver". In the lines that follow in Mechthild, the soul, nurtured by the omnitemporal mother, is revealed at last as the writer's individual being: "your breasts were so full that from one breast all at once seven rays streamed over my body and my soul".[51]

The most vital function of such transitions of imagery, however, is to convey the interdependence and interpenetration of the human and the divine. Thus (II 5–6) God and the soul become light, moisture and dress each for the other, when Mechthild says:

> Du lúhtest in die sele min
> als dú sunne gegen dem golde . . .
> Du kleidest dich mit der sele min
> und du bist ouch ir nehstes cleit.

> You gleam in my soul
> as the sun on gold . . .
> You clothe yourself with my soul,
> and you are its dress, next to the skin.

And God, in his reply:

> Swenne ich schine, so muost du lúhten;
> swenne ich vlússe, so muost du vúhten.

> If I shine, you must gleam,
> if I flow, you must be moist.[52]

The interdependence is such that, reversing the traditional image of the divine healer, the soul can even say (III 2): "My lord, if you'd take me home with you, I'd be your doctor forever". Such exchange is again evoked in its paradoxical quality in images of the mouth and the kiss: here (III 1) there is also a startling transition from "she"— the soul—to "I":

> Merke, ob si do út wart gekússet? In dem kusse wart si do ufgeruket in die höste höhi úber aller engel köre . . . Da sach ich die schöpfnisse und die ordenunge des gottes huses das er selber mit seinem munde hat gebuwen.

Look carefully: did she get kissed at all there? In the kiss she was impelled into the highest height, above all the choirs of angels . . . There I saw the creation and the ordering of God's house, which he himself built with his mouth.

Soon, when the image returns (III 5), the divine mouth, that both uttered the Word by which all was created and kissed the soul heavenwards, assumes the soul into itself:

> Do sprach der minnekliche munt,
> der mine sele hat durwunt . . .
> "Du bist miner gerunge ein minnevülunge,
> du bist miner brust ein süssú külunge,
> du bist ein kreftig kus mines mundes . . ."[53]

> Then spoke the loving mouth
> that wounded my soul with kissing . . .
> "You are a loving sensation of my desire,
> you are a sweet coolness of my breast,
> you are a passionate kiss of my mouth . . ."

In the most thrilling associative use of the imagery of the mouth (II 3), it is transformed into flight and music—a flight that is not *towards* God, as in the Platonic tradition, but *with* God, and a music that is human as much as divine:

> Der ungeteilet got . . . füllet si mit dem unlidigem ateme sines vliessenden mundes; und wie si gant ane arbeit als die vogele in dem lufte, so si keine vedren rürent . . .

> und wie dú gotheit clinget,
> dú mönscheit singet,
> der helig geist die liren des himelriches vingeret,
> das alle di seiten müssent clingen,
> die da gespannen sint in der minne.[54]

The undivided God . . . fills her with the painless breath of his flowing mouth, and effortlessly they move like birds in the air, no feather stirring . . .

and as the godhead sounds,
humanity sings,
the Holy Ghost fingers heaven's lyre
so that all the strings
must sound, made taut in love.

Related to the images of flight and music is that of the dance of the soul with God. It occurs first in the justly celebrated scene of divine union (I 44), in which Mechthild re-enacts and relives the rôle of the bride in the Song of Songs: "I cannot dance, my lord, unless you lead me . . ." Less well known is her darkly ironic, self-deprecating variation on the theme when she is older, in one of the later Books (IV 1):

O maget, was dir denne got wil geben!
Er wil dir ein schöne jungling wesen
und wil den himmelreigen mit dir tretten.
O ich unselig lammer hunt, ich húlze ouch mit dir![55]

Maiden, just think what God wants to give you!
For you he wants to be a beautiful young man,
and wants to tread the measure of the heavenly dance with you.
Oh cursed lame dog that I am—even with you I limp!

In Mechthild's dialogues between the soul and Minne, Love plays a rôle that ranges from servant to seductress to tyrannic empress: she can wait upon the soul, promise her all, yet without warning she can also rebuke, punish and torment. To cite from one such dialogue near the opening (I 3): the soul says to Minne:

Eya allerliebeste jungfrouwe,
nu hast du lange min kamererin gewesen,
nu sage mir, wie sol ich dar ane wesen?
Du hast mich gejagt, gevangen, gebunden
und so tief gewundet,
das ich niemer wirde gesunt.
Du hast mir manigen kúlenschlag geben,
sage mir, sol ich ze jungest vor dir genesen?

Wúrde ich nút getödet von diner hant,
so were mir bas, das ich dich nie hette bekant.

Die minne:

Das ich dich jagete, des luste mich;
das ich dich vieng, des gerte ich;
das ich dich bant, des fröwete ich mich;
do ich dich wundote, do wurde du mit mir vereinet;
so ich dir kúlinschlege gibe, so wirde ich din gewaltig . . .
wie wenest du snöder wurm mögen vor mir genesen?

Ah dearest of all maidens,
now that you've long been my chambermaid,
now tell me, where will this lead me?
You have hunted, captured, bound
and wounded me so deeply
that I'll never be well again.
You have clubbed me many times—
tell me, shall I be cured of you at last?
If I'm not to be killed at your hands,
it would be better for me if I'd never known you!

Minne:

Hunting you gave me delight,
capturing you was my desire,
binding you filled me with joy,
wounding you made you one with me,
clubbing you put you in my power . . .
How do you suppose, base worm, that you can be cured of me?

Even if Minne is disdainful, the soul longs for her still: Minne's dominance is frightening, inescapable—and ardently desired by her victim.

Soon afterwards the interdependence of the two figures is expressed in a luminous image, in which the soul says:

O minne, disen brief han ich us dinem munde geschriben:
nu gip mir, frowe, din ingesigel.

Oh Minne, I wrote this letter out of your mouth—
now, my lady, give me your seal.[56]

The love-letter is not from the one to the other, but is itself the two-in-one; the letter's seal is also the kiss of union. And yet, in that kiss, it is as if there were only one loving mouth, not two. In these dialogues Mechthild conveys the shifting perspectives—the inner uncertainties, helplessness, oppression and elation—perhaps more vividly than any direct confession, of Augustine's kind, could have done.

In Mechthild the poetic "I"—the representative or exemplary rôle of the protagonist—is seldom made explicit, except in those moments (more frequent in her later writing) where she defends her divine inspiration against attacks from hostile churchmen. In Marguerite Porete's work, such moments of defence, indeed defiance, come up often; but even more, her poetic "I" is pervasively present in the leitmotif of the "simple soul", the "free soul", which the empirical "I", Marguerite, aspires to be, and which she sees as having unanswerable claims on the official Church (Sainte Eglise la Petite, as she calls it), and on the world. The claims were of such magnificent *outrecuidance* that they led to her persecution and cruel martyrdom. I have discussed the content of these claims, and their modes of expression, in some detail elsewhere.[57] Here I shall illustrate from only one of Marguerite's exchanges between Love and Soul, which has not been singled out before for critical attention. It is characteristic in that, like most of her *Mirouer*, it consists of dialogues among allegorical figures, of whom L'Ame, Amour and Raison are the most prominent throughout the work. Characteristic too is the way that argument here moves towards the oasis of a lyrical moment:[58]

<Amour> O tres bien nee, dit Amour a ceste precieuse marguerite, bien soiez vous entree ou seul franc manoir, ouquel nul ne entre, se il n'est de vostre lygnage, sans bastardise.
Ceste Ame, dit Amour, est *aencree*[59] es habondances et affluences de divine amour ... l'amour de telle Ame est si conioincte aux

affluences du plus de celle oultre divine amour . . . Car tout ainsy, dit
Amour, comme le fer est vestu du feu et a la semblance perdue[60] de
luy, pource que le feu est le plus fort qui l'a mué[61] en luy, tout aussi
est ceste Ame vestue de ce plus et nourrie et muee en ce plus, pour
l'amour de ce plus, sans faire compte du moins . . . Ceste Ame ayme
en la doulce contree de oultre paix, par quoy il n'est rien qui puisse
aider ne grever a ceulx qui la ayment, ne creature creee, ne chose
donnee, ne rien que Dieu promecte.

Raison   Et quoy donc? dit Raison.

Amour   Ce qui oncques ne fut donné, ne n'est, ne ne sera, qui l'a fait
nue et l'a mis a nient . . .

L'Ame parle de son amy et si dit ainsi

> Il est, dit ceste Ame,
> ce ne luy fault mie,
> et je ne suis mie,
> et si ne me fault mie,
> 5   et si m'a paix donnee,
> et ne vifs sinon de paix
> qui est de ses dons nee[62]
> en mon ame, sans pensee,
> et si ne puis nient
> 10   se il ne m'est donné.[63]

<Amour>   Oh highborn one, says Love to this precious Marguerite,
welcome in the sole noble manor, which none enters who is not of
your lineage, without bastardy.
This Soul, says Love, is anchored in the abounding floods of divine
love . . . the love of such a Soul is conjoined to the floods of the more
of this divine love beyond love . . . For, says Love, as iron is clothed
by fire and has lost the semblance of iron, since fire, being stronger,
has transmuted it into itself—even so this Soul is clothed by this
more, nurtured and transmuted into this more, for love of this more,
without reckoning the less . . . This Soul loves in the sweet region of
peace beyond peace; thus there's nothing that can help or harm those
who love there—neither created being nor anything that's given, nor
anything God promises.

Raison   And what then? says Reason.

Amour That which was never given, nor is, nor shall be, which has made her naked and set her at naught . . .

L'Ame (speaks of her lover and says)

> He is—says this Soul—
> he is in want of nothing,
> and I am nothing,
> and am in want of nothing,
> 5   and this has given me peace,
> and I live just from the peace
> which is born of his gifts
> in my soul, without thought,
> and I can do nothing
> 10   if he's not given to me.

As Dante and his poet-friends allude to the "gentle heart" *(cor gentil)*[64]—the heart informed by that inner nobility which distinguishes the élite of human love—so Marguerite imagines her "free souls" as an élite, an unblemished aristocracy of divine love. Amour, in her greeting to the Soul, plays on Marguerite's name: "Marguerite" is the empirical "I", but also the pearl of great price *(pretiosa margarita:* Matthew 13, 46), for which the divine lover has paid all he has. Then Amour echoes and develops one of her earlier images in the work (28), of the Soul swimming in the sea of joy that flows from divinity: "for she herself is that joy, and swims and floats in joy without feeling joy, for she dwells in joy and joy in her". Here, however, she is anchored in the divine floods—steadfast and serene. The image is taken in other, intellectually more demanding, directions. The expressions *oultre divine* and *oultre paix,* and the simile of iron transmuted into fire, indicate that, whether directly or through an intermediary, Marguerite had come to know the language of Dionysius, Maximus and Eriugena.[65] But she varies it in unexpected ways. She transforms "the more" *(le plus)* into floods of transcending love. The iron and fire image of neoplatonic tradition expressed the soul's union with God; here, more startlingly, as iron is clothed by fire, so her Soul is clothed by "the more": the Dionysian concept of a state beyond being (ὑπερούσιος) is called up with new vividness. Finally, Amour's image of the Soul made naked by the divine presence corresponds to Mechthild's Song of Songs fantasy (*Fliessendes Licht*, I 44), where God, at the moment of love-union, bids her to undress, to cast off fear and shame and every outer virtue.[66] But here in the Soul's answer, which takes on lyrical colouring and movement, Marguerite extends this into an expression of complete transcendence—lover and beloved share the nothingness beyond being—that nonetheless includes a touching human dependence on the beloved's part: "I live just from the peace / which is born of his gifts".

I do not wish to overstress the affinities between these two mystical *prosimetra* and the *Vita Nuova*. In many obvious ways Dante's *is* a different imaginative realm. Dante's literary point of departure for the *Vita Nuova* was the realm of the *vidas* and *razos* of the troubadour Uc de San Circ (cf. chap. III, pp. 66–70). Among these, Uc had included a brief, stylised even if not wholly fictive, autobiographical *vida*, together with *razos* for two of his own songs—that is, biographical prose explanations, longer and more specific than the songs themselves, of the circumstances in which he had come to compose them. So too Dante in the *Vita Nuova* was, we might say, writing *razos* for a group of his own early lyrics, though also composing fresh lyrics for his new ensemble of poetry and prose. Yet what gives the *Vita Nuova* a dimension, a seriousness and magnetic power that leave the world of Uc de San Circ far behind is precisely the presence of qualities that take it towards the spiritual world of Mechthild and Marguerite. Dante's, like theirs, is essentially an inner world, where love is imagined and celebrated with boundless intensity, and where the sublimation of the erotic motifs is directed towards a more sublime mode of understanding, one that involves the empirical "I" totally.

It is not a question of direct influence. I know that many scholars (especially German ones) have speculated about Dante's knowledge of Mechthild, and have been tempted to see in her the prototype of the figure Matelda in Dante's earthly paradise. But this is a temptation that I think should be resisted: the transmission of the Latin version of her *Fliessendes Licht* is too late and too scanty to make it at all plausible.[67] The text that acted as intellectual midwife for the young Dante, helping him to move from the brief trivial *razos* of Uc de San Circ's kind to a work of the scale and ambitions of the *Vita Nuova*, was a different *prosimetrum:* Boethius' *Consolation of Philosophy.* We know from Dante himself, in his *Convivio,* that he read the *Consolation* soon after Beatrice's death. This is the work *par excellence* that will have introduced him to a paradigm of the sublimation of pain and loss, and to the process of attaining an exalted mode of understanding—not so much the scholastic kind of understanding, that Dante was also beginning to master at this time, as an individual, personally mediated kind.

The first time that Amore appears to Dante, in his sleep (III), there is no dialogue: only the god speaks. His utterances, like those of the spirits within Dante's soul when Beatrice was first revealed to him (II), are in Latin: the words, awesome and numinous, stand out from the vernacular that surrounds them, and are for the most part incomprehensible to the dreamer. Amore is holding outstretched a figure whom Dante in his vision comes to recognise as Beatrice:

> ne le sue parole dicea molte cose, le quali io non intendea se non poche; tra le quali intendea queste: *"Ego dominus tuus".* Ne le sue braccia mi parea vedere una persona dormire nuda, salvo che involta mi parea in uno drappo sanguigno leggeramente . . . E ne l'una de le mani mi parea che questi tenesse una cosa la quale ardesse tutta, e pareami che mi dicesse queste parole: *"Vide cor tuum".* E quando elli era stato alquanto, pareami che disvegliasse questa che dormia; e tanto si sforzava per suo ingegno, che le facea mangiare questa cosa che in mano li ardea, la quale ella mangiava dubitosamente. Appresso ciò poco dimorava che la sua letizia si convertia in amarissimo pianto; e così piangendo, si ricogliea questa donna ne le sue braccia, e con essa mi parea che si ne gisse verso il cielo.

> . . . in his words he said many things that I did not understand, save for a few; among them I understood these: *"I am your lord".* In his arms it seemed to me I saw a figure sleeping, naked, except that she seemed to me to be wrapped lightly in a cloth the colour of blood . . . And in one of his hands it seemed to me he held something that was all ablaze, and it seemed to me that he said these words to me: *"Behold your heart".* And when he had waited a while, it seemed to me he awoke her who was sleeping; and he used such skilful effort that he made her eat what was blazing in his hand—she ate it apprehensively. A few moments later, his joy turned into bitterest weeping; and

weeping thus he gathered this lady in his arms, and with her, it seemed to me, he made his way heavenward.

The relating of the vision is at the same time harrowing and analytic: with the refrainlike *mi parea* Dante stresses over and over again that he is recording punctiliously, that this is how, in the vision, it appeared or seemed to him. In the sonnet that Dante then composes describing his vision, there is only one such word of seeming *(sembrava):* the poetic account is, paradoxically, both more direct and less explicit, the language more restrained, the piercing oneiric evocations now accommodated to an existing, more decorous diction and imaginative horizon. Dante sends his sonnet, he tells, to many *trovatori,* asking them to interpret, to judge. He was as it were presenting his poetic credentials; it was the beginning of his individual myth of the new life, as poet and as Beatrice's votary.

Dante's dialogue with Amore does not take place before the god's third appearance (XII). The events leading up to this—once more narrated in prose—are, in their plot-mechanism, typical of the troubadour *razos* of Provence. Fearing that his love for Beatrice might be discovered, Dante ostensibly directs his attentions first to one young woman, then to another, making these the screen *(schermo)* and protection *(difesa)* for his veritable love. With the second, Dante unwittingly overdoes it, and gossip about this reaches Beatrice, who then one day passes Dante and refuses to greet him.

What makes the atmosphere of this incident wholly different from that of the lightly told anecdotes in the *razos* is the solemnity and spirituality with which Dante invests his passion. He sees Beatrice as "the destroyer of all vices and the queen of the virtues" (X). By a wordplay, her *salute* is for Dante both greeting and salvation: "in it dwelt all my beatitude" (X); "when she appeared . . . a flame of charity arose in me, that made me pardon whoever had offended me" (XI). Overcome with grief at losing the beatitude Beatrice had denied him, praying for mercy to her and to Amore, Dante falls asleep, crying like a beaten child. This time the apparition of the god, at Dante's bedside, is evoked in prose that carries deliberate echoes of Boethius.[68] Here too the visitant is not recognised at first, and, like Philosophia, laments the narrator's pitiable state. His first words, once more in Latin, are augustly mystifying:

> *"Fili mi, tempus est ut pretermictantur simulacra nostra".* Allora mi parea che io lo conoscesse, però che mi chiamava così come assai fiate ne li miei sonni m'avea già chiamato: e riguardandolo, parvemi che piangesse pietosamente, e parea che attendesse da me alcuna parola; ond'io, assicurandomi, cominciai a parlare così con esso: "Segnore de la nobiltade, e perché piangi tu?" E quelli mi dicea queste parole: *"Ego tanquam centrum circuli, cui simili modo se habent circumferentie partes; tu autem non sic".*[69]

> *"My son, it is time for our semblances to be cast aside".* Then it seemed to me that I knew him, because he was addressing me as he had already done many a time in my dreams: and looking at him, it seemed to me he wept compassionately, and it seemed that he expected some word of reply from me; so, taking courage, I began to speak with him thus: "Lord of nobility, why are you weeping?" And he said these words to me: *"I am like the centre of the circle, to which all parts of the circumference stand in similar relation; but you are not like that".*

The contrast between Amore and the dreamer is heightened by the contrast of languages. Amore's realm is changeless, like Philosophia's; yet like her he can also show sorrow and pity for one who is caught in the toils of change; and he can dispel Dante's anguish as Philosophia dispels that of the imprisoned Boethius. At first, however, Dante, like Boethius, portrays himself as too troubled in spirit to comprehend his mentor's words. For a moment the dialogue with Amore goes almost to the brink of comedy, as he asks: "Why is it, my lord, that you speak to me with such obscurity?" Thereupon the god relents and replies more lucidly, in the vernacular, advising Dante to send a poem to Beatrice which he, Amore, will accompany. When he awakes, Dante composes a ballata: the whole is addressed to the ballata itself, personified: she is to be his mediatrix. The device enables him both to project his inner drama and to explain to Beatrice that his love has never wavered. The sorrows with which the vision had begun are forgotten, and a light-hearted element enters, as when the poet says to his persona, the poem:

Sed ella non ti crede,
dì che domandi Amor, che sa lo vero.

If she doesn't believe you,
tell her to ask Amor, who knows the truth.

As before Dante had adopted the ruse of courting two other ladies, in order to screen and to protect his unique love, so now his ruse is to have two intermediaries—the love-god, and the ballata—to woo Beatrice for him.

It is not till after far more anguished and exalted moments—Dante's delirium, in which he has the premonition of Beatrice's death and himself begs to die (XXIII), and his celebration of Beatrice as an epiphany of heavenly love, heralded by Giovanna (his friend Cavalcanti's beloved) as Christ was heralded by Giovanni (XXIV)—that Dante turns aside and, speaking as a critic, explains that to personify Amore, or a ballata, is simply a poetic licence, a rhetorical figure sanctioned by the classical poets (XXV). After moments that had been presented with compelling visionary power, why this sudden cool reflection and distancing? We might surmise that the distancing has hidden motives—that the thought-processes behind the rhetorical figures had been too painfully real to treat direct. Yet this excursus does not stand alone: it belongs with the numerous structural commentaries on his poems that Dante furnishes throughout the work: "First I divide this canzone into three parts . . . The first part can be divided into four . . . The second part into two . . .", the second of which is again twice subdivided (XIX)—as if Dante were not a lover but an industrious Dominican in Santa Maria Novella, articulating a text of Aristotle's.

Dante's analytic procedures remind me of a memorable phrase of T. S. Eliot's: "the more perfect the artist, the more completely separate in him will be the man who suffers and the mind which creates".[70] By his analyses, Dante is in effect saying: These poems are *not* my inner life, they are consciously crafted artefacts. Look: first I do this, then I do that . . .

The poems always remain very deliberately detached from the surrounding prose—prose that creates both the effect of immediacy, by supplying a background of purported inner autobiography, and the effect of distance, by supplying rhetorical exegesis. Dante wants both to distance and to bridge the distance: the poems are, and are not, he. In just this way, too, Mechthild and Marguerite use their many articulations, enumerations and divisions of states of mind and feeling, not only in their chapter-headings but in the very fabric of their prose. This is what gives their poetic "I" a certain objectivity and exemplary force that the empirical "I" alone cannot have. As the young Dante wanted to be remembered not as an infatuated dreamer but as a poet, so Mechthild and Marguerite wanted to be remembered not as women who had abnormal experiences but as prophets, *vates* who had something unparalleled to teach posterity.

After Beatrice's death, even if Dante, the empirical "I", was consoled in his sorrow by a gentle lady who gazed at him from a window (XXXV), who had a look and colouring that reminded him of his beloved (XXXVII)—and who had not yet been transformed into a personification of Philosophy, by the poetic "I" of the *Convivio*[71]—Dante's cult of Beatrice as a heavenly being, channel of grace and salvation to her devotee, became more real than ever before.[72] The final sonnet in the *Vita Nuova, Oltre la spera che più larga gira* (XLI), "commissioned" by two gentle ladies, evokes Beatrice as one of the blessed souls in the empyrean, beyond the highest of the circling heavens, the crystalline. Dante's thought, still filled with sorrow, rises to her there, where she is honoured among the saints and sheds her radiance on his spirit. Yet he is dazzled: even if "the peregrine spirit" *(lo peregrino spirito)* can contemplate her miraculous nature, this remains beyond the reach of the empirical "I"—

> Vedela tal, che quando 'l mi ridice,
> io no lo intendo, sì parla sottile
> al cor dolente, che lo fa parlare.
> So io che parla di quella gentile,
> però che spesso ricorda Beatrice,
> sì ch'io lo 'ntendo ben, donne mie care.

> He sees her such that, when he repeats this to me,
> I do not comprehend it—so subtly does he speak
> to the grieving heart, that makes him speak.
> I know he is speaking of that gentle one,

because he often mentions Beatrice—
so then, dear ladies, I comprehend him well.

Dante's spirit, descending from the heavenly height, brings Beatrice's name back repeatedly into his earthly existence, and thereby brings him a vestige of understanding of the heavenly.

The effect of this newly-won understanding is seen, I would suggest, in the final passage of prose that follows (XLII):

> Appresso questo sonetto apparve a me una mirabile visione, ne la quale io vidi cose che mi fecero proporre di non dire più di questa benedetta infino a tanto che io potesse più degnamente trattare di lei. E di venire a ciò io studio quanto posso, sì com'ella sae veracemente . . .

> After this sonnet a miraculous vision appeared to me, in which I saw things that made me resolve to say no more about this blessed one till I could treat of her more fittingly. And to arrive at that point I strive as much as I can, as she truly knows . . .

The phrase *apparve a me una mirabile visione* takes us back to the beginning of the work, when "a gentle sleep befell me, in which a marvellous vision appeared to me" *(mi sopragiunse uno soave sonno, ne lo quale m'apparve una maravigliosa visione)*[73]—the vision that was Amore's first epiphany, when he bade Beatrice eat Dante's heart. In a sense this brings the *Vita Nuova* full circle—yet note the differences. The first vision is marvellous, or amazing, and comes in a dream; the last is miraculous, and, for the one-and-only time in the work, it is what it is. Every previous vision had been given "in sleep" or "in imagination"; the final vision is real. Neither Mechthild nor Marguerite ever presents her visionary experience as dreams—neither ever suggests that she slept when visions came to her, or that she merely imagined them. The visions were too vital for that. If they had been only literary fantasies about personified beings, they could never have had the binding strength which the poetic "I" claims for them.

In each of the writers alluded to in this chapter, the poetic "I" makes claims that go beyond those of the empirical "I". Dhuoda is an instructress as well as a sufferer; Rather is "the last of the just" as well as a troublemaker mocked as mad; Mechthild and Marguerite are charismatic proclaimers of divine union as well as anguished souls; Dante is the celebrant of a new saint as well as an overwrought young man in the pangs of dispriz'd love. It is not as though the one "I" belonged to the prose and the other to the verse: both verse and prose have manifold functions for all these writers of *prosimetra*. Yet the alternation between prose and verse is always bound up, in more complex, less predictable ways, with the authors' strategies of shifts of perspective, shifts of voice, shifts of the "I", shifts in the ways the authors see themselves—in their means towards self-discovery.

These fluctuations are an essential aspect of the poetics of the genre. They are less apparent in Dante's later return to the mixed form, his unfinished *Convivio*. There the philosophical prose arguments that Dante develops out of his canzoni are largely confined to the didactic; the works considered here, by contrast, are protean. For me the three vernacular *prosimetra* of the late thirteenth century—*Das fliessende Licht, Le mirouer des simples ames, Vita Nuova*—represent the summits of achievement. I do not know if the centuries that followed ever again brought to the mixed form such shining individualities.

Notes
Index

Notes

1. *Petrolio* was published by Einaudi, Turin; the passage cited is on p. 3. The triple "etcetera" corresponds to "ecc." in the original.

I Menippean Elements

1. See below, chap. III, p. 54–59.

2. Ed. Ludwig Rockinger, *Briefsteller und Formelbücher des elften bis vierzehnten Jahrhunderts* (Munich, 1863–1864), I, 53–88 (for the definition and account of the *prosimetrum,* see pp. 54–55). On the date of Hugh's treatise, cf. Tore Janson, *Prose Rhythm in Medieval Latin* (Stockholm, 1975), p. 78. An anonymous later *dictator,* from Austria, cites Boethius' *Consolatio Philosophiae* as his example of *prosimetricum dictamen* (Rockinger, II, 726). The editorial staff of *Mittellateinisches Wörterbuch* and *Thesaurus Linguae Latinae* have kindly confirmed for me (in a letter of 17.9.92) that they have no instances of the word *prosimetrum* among their materials.

3. As Karsten Friis-Jensen, *Saxo Grammaticus as Latin Poet* (Rome, 1987), p. 30, notes: "Unfortunately no survey of the medieval Latin *prosimetrum* exists". He himself makes valuable observations on a number of prosimetric texts (ibid., pp. 29–36), and refers to the excursus on prosimetric form in Udo Kindermann's dissertation, *Laurentius von Durham. Consolatio de morte amici* (Erlangen-Nuremberg, 1969), pp. 56–82. Among texts of literary interest which are not discussed in the present book and are not mentioned by either Friis-Jensen or Kindermann, I would signal particularly Ennodius, *Paraenesis didascalica ad Ambrosium et Beatum (Opera,* ed. Friedrich Vogel, *MGH,* Berlin, 1885, pp. 310–315); some of the epistolary *prosimetra* of the twelfth century, including the *Epistolae duorum amantium,* ed. Ewald Könsgen (Leiden-Cologne, 1974), the *Epistolae ad amicum,* ed. Marvin L. Colker, *Analecta Dublinensia* (Cambridge, Mass., 1975), pp. 63–178, and Guido of Bazoches's *Liber epistularum,* ed. Herbert Adolfs-

son (Stockholm, 1969); and, last not least, Godfrey of Viterbo's huge and many-faceted *Pantheon* (partial ed. by Georg Waitz, *MGH, Scriptores* XXII, Berlin, 1872, 107–307). It is noteworthy, too, that verses, both cited and freshly composed, were at times interspersed in the prose of scientific treatises, such as Dicuil's *Liber de mensura orbis terrae,* ed. and tr. J. J. Tierney (Dublin, 1967)—for the later period, cf. Lynn Thorndike, "Unde versus", *Traditio* 11 (1955), 162–193.

4. "Note on the Poetic and the Empirical 'I' in Medieval Authors", in his *Romanische Literaturstudien* (Tübingen, 1959), pp. 100–112.

5. *Anatomy of Criticism* (Princeton, 1957), p. 308.

6. Ibid., p. 309.

7. Ibid., p. 311.

8. Mikhail Bakhtin, *Problems of Dostoevsky's Poetics,* tr. R. W. Rotsel (Michigan, 1973), pp. 87–113.

9. Ibid., pp. 94–95.

10. Heinrich Dörrie, author of the entry "Menippos von Gadara" in *Der Kleine Pauly,* III, 1217, suggests that Menippus' slavery may have been invented in order to make him appear more like Diogenes.

11. Cited in Diogenes Laertius, *Vitae Philosophorum* VI, 29–30 (ed. H. S. Long, Oxford, 1964). With three brief exceptions (the lines from Bakhtin cited at n. 9 above, the phrase from Seneca at n. 34 below, and the Aristophanic verses at chap. II, n. 28), all translations throughout this book are my own.

12. Cicero, *Academica* I, ii, 9.

13. Jean-Pierre Cèbe, *Varron, Satires Ménippées: Édition, traduction et commentaire* (Rome, 1972–: fascs. 1–9, 1972–1990), Fragm. 44, p. 188. While *repuerascere* is found already in Plautus, *puellascere* is Varro's own formation. The fragments alluded to below are cited and numbered according to Cèbe's edition.

14. Ibid., pp. 493–499.

15. Ibid., pp. 196–205.

16. *Soliloquia* I, 1.

17. See below, chap. II, pp. 40–41.

18. See below, chap. II, pp. 46–52.

19. *Dialogus: Patrologia Latina* 157, 535–706.

20. Ed. Charles Burnett, *Studi medievali,* ser. 3, 25 (1984), 857–894.

21. See especially the fine commentary by Francisco Rico, *Vida u Obra de Petrarca I: Lectura del Secretum* (Padua, 1974).

22. Petronius died in 66 A.D.; the papyrus containing the *Iolaus* fragment was copied in the second century A.D.

23. "A Greek *Satyricon?*", *Bulletin of the Institute of Classical Studies* 18 (1971), 53–68. Specialists will see at once how deeply indebted the next paragraph is to Parsons' suggestions.

Since Parsons' work on the *Iolaus* fragment, a second such text has come to light in a papyrus of the second century A.D.: the "Narrative about Tinouphis in Prosimetrum" published and discussed by M. W. Haslam in *Papyri Greek and Egyptian* (London, 1981), pp. 35–45. The lines that are intelligible concern a prophet or magus, Tinouphis, and his miraculous escape from death, an executioner (who is probably a slave called Sosias), and an adulteress. Even if the extant fragments of *Iolaus* and *Tinouphis* are younger than the *Satyricon,* it now seems virtually certain that Petronius must have had Greek precedents for a prosimetric narrative with satiric or erotic or sensational elements. Compare Raymond Astbury, "Petronius, P.Oxy. 3010 [i.e. *Iolaus*], and Menippean Satire", *Classical Philology* 72 (1977), 22–31; Astbury, however, overstates his case in denying any relation between Petronius and the Menippea of Varro and Seneca.

24. At line 21 of the fragment, Parsons in his note proposes the apt completion νεκ[ρὸν] ἄταφο[ν, though he does not include it in his text.

25. Parsons (p. 55) glosses τέλειος as "unmutilated". But a sense such as "consummately trained" would probably fit the context better here.

Since Parson's presentation of 1971, Reinhold Merkelbach (*Zeitschrift für Papyrologie und Epigraphik* 11 [1973], 81–100) has suggested that in the Sotadean verses the "mystic" makes a series of allusions to Iolaus' escapades, so as to bring him to utter a full confession of these and clear himself, as a ritual preliminary to being received into the mysteries of the *galli.* Merkelbach sees in the fragment "a dense web of satiric allusion to mystery-like ceremonies" (p. 100). In a note added in Parsons' second publication of the fragment, in *The Oxyrhynchos Papyri* XLII (1974), 34–41, at p. 35, n. 1, E. R. Dodds suggests an outline for the plot, seeing it as comparable to that in Terence's *Eunuchus:* Iolaus, hoping to "screw by stealth" (30), has planned to enter his beloved's house in the guise of a eunuch *gallus,* and, in order to get his impersonation right, has sent a friend to learn the details from a real *gallus.* According to Dodds, the friend in his Sotadean verses gives "some specimens of the jargon he has learned (hence the odd mixture of religious and vulgar language)". While Merkelbach's and Dodds' suggestions are illuminating, neither seems compatible with every detail in the fragment: in particular, neither can easily account for the precise force of the friend's phrase to Iolaus, "that *you are going to* screw by stealth" (ὅτι δόλῳ σὺ βεινεῖν μέλλεις). Preparation for a confession of past misdeeds could hardly include plans for future sinning; nor can the phrase be simply a specimen of learnt mystic jargon. Here the friend's words must rather show him as an accomplice fully involved in Iolaus' intrigue and projected sexual adventure—perhaps even (if we pursue Dodds' conjecture) in a rôle like that of Parmeno in Terence's play (cf. *Eun.* 568–578).

26. All references to the *Satyricon* below are to the "Tusculum" edition: Petronius, *Satyrica,* ed. Konrad Müller, tr. Wilhelm Ehlers, 3rd ed. (Munich, 1983). On *debattuere,* cf. J. N. Adams, *The Latin Sexual Vocabulary* (London, 1982), pp. 147, 215.

27. References below are to Seneca, *Apocolocyntosis,* ed. and tr. P. T. Eden (Cambridge, 1984). This title for Seneca's work, which is commonly adopted by editors but the precise import of which is still disputed, occurs in no manuscript but is recorded by the Greek-writing historian Dio Cassius.

28. Cf. M. D. Reeve, "Apotheosis . . . per saturam", *Classical Philology* 79 (1984), 305–307.

29. Iohannes Immonides, *Cena Cypriani,* ed. Karl Strecker, *Poetae Latini Aevi Carolini* IV (*MGH,* Berlin, 1881), 857–900, at p. 899.

30. Ibid., p. 870.

31. Ibid., p. 900.

32. Cf. especially *Antapodosis* IV, 12, ed. and tr. Albert Bauer, Reinhold Rau, *Quellen zur Geschichte der Sächsischen Kaiserzeit,* 2nd ed. (Darmstadt, 1977), pp. 244–495, at pp. 414–416.

33. *Legatio* 31, ibid., pp. 524–589, at p. 550. The translators render *ludi* here as "Schauspiele"; *Novum Glossarium,* s.v., cites this passage as referring to mystery-plays.

34. *Apocol.* 4, 3 (for this phrase I cite P. T. Eden's translation).

35. In what follows I refer to the edition by M. A. D'Avezac, *Éthicus et les ouvrages cosmographiques intitulés de ce nom* (Paris, 1852): his text (ibid., pp. 231–317) is considerably more lucid than that, more frequently cited, of Heinrich Wuttke, *Die Kosmographie des Istrier Aithikos* (Leipzig, 1853). A new edition, by Otto Prinz for the *MGH,* is in preparation (see p. 142).

36. The name means "moral philosopher" (i.e. *ethicus*), but throughout the work "Aethicus" is used as a proper name.

37. Some modern scholars ascribe the *Cosmographia* to the Irish Bishop Virgil (i.e. Fergil) of Salzburg, who died in 784: cf. esp. *Virgil von Salzburg, Missionar und Gelehrter,* ed. Heinz Dopsch, Roswitha Juffinger (Salzburg, 1985). But the fact that the earliest known manuscript of the work was copied already in 754 (see Michael Herren, "Wozu dient die Fälschung der Kosmographie des Aethicus?", in *Lateinische Kultur im VIII. Jahrhundert,* ed. Albert Lehner, Walter Berschin (St. Ottilien, 1989, p. 145), makes this attribution at least questionable.

38. W. M. Lindsay, "Columba's *Altus* and the *Abstrusa Glossary*", *Classical Quarterly* 17 (1923), 197–199.

39. Cf. Kurt Hillkowitz, *Zur Kosmographie des Aethicus, Teil II* (Frankfurt am Main, 1973), p. 9. ("Teil I" of this work is Hillkowitz's *Dissertation,* Cologne, 1934).

40. The caesurae are always marked by a colon in the text of F. J. H. Jenkinson, *The Hisperica Famina* (Cambridge, 1908)—see also Jenkinson's

observations on caesura, ibid., pp. xvii–xix; they are not marked in the more recent edition by Michael Herren, *The Hisperica Famina I: The A-Text* (Toronto, 1974).

41. I.e. the pirates are as swift and savage as eagles. The phrase echoes Isaiah 40, 31: *qui autem sperant in Domino mutabunt fortitudinem, assument pennas sicut* aquilae.

42. D'Avezac, p. 253, with my own line-arrangement and punctuation. For the words *aulonis, brumericus, cacemphatus,* and *catago,* see *Mittellateinisches Wörterbuch,* s.v. *Nauclerium,* if my translation of it as gen. pl. is correct, presupposes an otherwise unattested form **naucleris.* The accusative *singultum* (where one might expect abl. *singultu*) is also problematic, but neither edition gives a variant reading.

43. Cf. Vernam Hull, ed., *Longes Mac N-Uislenn. The Exile of the Sons of Uisliu* (New York, 1949), pp. 27–28; Rudolf Thurneysen, *Die irische Helden- und Königsage* (Halle, 1921), pp. 54–56. Of particular interest in relation to the passages in the *Cosmographia* are Thurneysen's observations (p. 54) on the "lockere syntaktische Fügung" in the *retoirics,* and that "manchmal scheint ein gewisser Parallelismus der Glieder angestrebt, so dass sie an die kirchlichen Sequenzen erinnern".

44. D'Avezac, p. 305.

45. Ibid., p. 266: *ea metrico et prosaico stylo graecis characteribus distinxit in enigmate rhethorico.* I am assuming that the variant *prosaico,* given in D'Avezac's apparatus, is correct: the reading in his text, *metrico et prosodico,* results in a pleonasm.

46. Philostratus, *The Life of Apollonius of Tyana,* III, 16–50.

47. D'Avezac, p. 240.

48. Ibid., p. 242.

49. Ibid., p. 243 (reading *habere* with the MSS).

50. Ibid., pp. 244–245.

51. Herren, "Fälschung" (cit. n. 37), p. 155.

52. D'Avezac, p. 274.

53. Ibid., p. 283.

54. Ibid., p. 292.

55. Ibid., p. 316.

56. Max Manitius, *Geschichte der lateinischen Literatur des Mittelalters,* I (Munich, 1911), 233.

57. See the admirable study and edition by Wolfram von den Steinen, *Notker der Dichter und seine geistige Welt* (2 vols., Berne, 1948).

58. See Walter Berschin, "Notkers Metrum de vita S. Galli", in *Florilegium Sangallense, Festschrift für Johannes Duft* (St. Gallen-Sigmaringen, 1980), pp. 71–121, at p. 81. All citations below are from Berschin's edition. Roughly contemporary with Notker's work is the *Vita Sanctae Aldegundis* by Hucbald of Saint-Amand (*Patrologia Latina* 132, 857–876), which contains a very small number of incidental verses (seven leonine hexameters in

chap. 3, and two in chap. 5), and hence can hardly be reckoned a fully-fledged *prosimetrum*. As a scholar, however, Hucbald was well-versed in earlier prosimetric tradition: not only does he utilise Martianus Capella and Boethius in his writings on music, but he is known to have owned a copy of Seneca's *Ludus* (cf. P. T. Eden, *Apocolocyntosis,* pp. 19–20).

59. Berschin, pp. 93–94. Strictly, *lyrico* in the second verse goes with *carmine* in the fourth ("you surpass the ancient poets in lyrical composition").

60. This strophe occurs in what Berschin (following von den Steinen) has rightly distinguished as a separate poem (inc. *Care, quid linguam taciturnus abdis*).

61. Berschin, p. 95; cf. Horace, *Carm.* II, 5, 1–3.

62. Berschin, pp. 96–97.

63. Ibid., p. 84.

64. Gustavo Vinay, *Alto medioevo latino* (Naples, 1978), p. 357.

65. Berschin, p. 98. The remainder of the work—which includes a long and serious sermon in prose put in the mouth of Gallus—survives in much more fragmentary form than the prelude that is sketched above.

66. *Analecta Dublinensia. Three Medieval Latin Texts in the Library of Trinity College Dublin* (Cambridge, Mass., 1975), pp. 179–235.

67. Ibid., p. 186.

68. *De nugis curialium,* III, 2.

69. *Analecta,* p. 213 (with verbal correspondences to Petronius italicised):

Hec quidem dumtaxat ex *equestri* querit ordine quod ardeat, illa vero sumit ab extrema plebe quo *caleat.* Huius *estuantis desiderium* sola *servitus accendit . . . Quedam* solis *sordibus* fervescit, nec . . . calescit *nisi vel* squalentes *servos vel cinctos alcius stratores* inspexerit. Venerias *harena* quam plures ad araturas impellit. Hec *mulioni pulvere perfuso* molliter succumbit, illam flexibilis et saltans *histrio* furere facit.

One woman seeks an object for her passion solely in the ranks of knights, another finds arousal among the lowest plebs. Her desire is kindled only by a slave . . . There's a woman who burns only for what's low, who doesn't . . . grow hot unless she looks at squalid slaves or grooms wearing their tunics too short. It's the arena that impels a lot of women to be arable venerially. One woman melts before a mule-driver smothered in dust, an actor, flexible and leaping, drives another woman wild.

The twelfth-century author has enriched his Petronian language by additional wordplay *(annominatio)—harena . . . araturas; mulioni . . . molliter—* for which I have tried to find approximate equivalents in translation. Note also his expression *cinctos alcius stratores,* where Petronius has *statores altius cinctos:* this could be a deliberate authorial change, but could equally reflect a scribal corruption or a confusion between the words *stator* and *strator.*

70. *Consolatio Philosophiae* III, pr. 2, 2. Citations are based on Ludwig Bieler's edition (*Corpus Christianorum,* Series Latina, 94, 1957).

71. Ibid., III, m. 2, 1–3:

> Quantas rerum flectat habenas
> Natura potens, quibus immensum
> legibus orbem provida servet . . .

72. *Analecta,* p. 214:

> Felices Natura vices secernere castis
> sancta solet. Quibus ad Venerem si laxet habenas,
> dat tamen attractis motam compescere frenis.

It was not till these pages were in press that two friends drew my attention to H. K. Riikonen's essay, *Menippean Satire as a Literary Genre, with special reference to Seneca's Apocolocyntosis* (Societas Scientiarum Fennica, Commentationes Humanarum Litterarum 83, Helsinki, 1987). This contains a series of theoretical reflections on Menippea, alluding to a wide range of texts ancient and modern, as well as to the ideas of Bakhtin and Frye. The bibliography (pp. 53–55) is especially valuable for secondary literature that goes beyond the classical range, including a work of reference: Eugene P. Kirk's *Menippean Satire: An Annotated Catalogue of Texts and Criticism* (New York, 1980).

II *Allegory and the Mixed Form*

1. See above, chap. I, n. 26.

2. *Sat.* 3, 2, citing Cicero, *Pro Caelio,* 41.

3. *De nuptiis Philologiae et Mercurii,* ed. James Willis (Leipzig, 1983); my citations are based on this edition, with the exceptions noted below.

4. *Cons.* II, m. 8, 29–30 (*amor / quo caelum regitur*). In the first line cited below, *semina . . . pugnantia* is echoed in Boethius, *Cons.* II, m. 8, 3; in the third, *elementa ligas* is echoed ibid., III, m. 9, 10.

5. *De nuptiis* 1. On the medieval exegesis of this passage, see esp. my discussion in *Fabula: Explorations into the Uses of Myth in Medieval Platonism* (Leiden-Cologne, 1974), chap. III and Appendix B.

6. I adopt the emendation *decurvatum,* proposed by R. G. M. Nisbet, noted in Danuta Shanzer's *Philosophical and Literary Commentary on Martianus Capella's De Nuptiis Philologiae et Mercurii Book I* (Berkeley-Los

Angeles-London, 1986), p. 52; the editions have *decuriatum*. I also retain Adolf Dick's ὑμνολογίζεις (cf. Shanzer, ibid.).

On the opening verses, and their contrast with the prose, there are also some stimulating observations in Fanny LeMoine, *Martianus Capella: A Literary Re-evaluation* (Munich, 1972), pp. 21–39. Yet I would concur with Danuta Shanzer's comment (p. 47): "Her treatment, however, must be used with care, since it is excessively subjective".

7. Cf. Shanzer, *Commentary*, p. 55.

8. *In Isagogen Porphyrii Commenta, Editio prima*, ed. Samuel Brandt (*Corpus Script. Eccl. Lat.* 48, 1906), p. 132, 3; cf. also *Index nominum et rerum*, s.v. "Petronius", ibid., p. 353.

9. *Cons.* I, m. 1, 1–11.

10. Bieler, *ad loc.*, notes Vergil, *Georg.* IV, 564–565; Horace, *Carm.* II, 9, 9; [ps–?] Seneca, *Octavia* 329 f; Prudentius, *Perist.* XI, 194; Ovid, *Ex Ponto* I, 4, 19 f.

11. *Cons.* I, pr. 1, 8–9.

12. Méthode d'Olympe, *Le Banquet*, ed. Herbert Musurillo, tr. Victor-Henry Debidour (*Sources Chrétiennes* 95, 1963).

13. *Symp.* 293 (*Le Banquet*, p. 322).

14. *Le Banquet*, p. 44, n. 1.

15. *Symp.* 11 (*Le Banquet*, p. 54).

16. *Cons.* I, pr. 1, 2.

17. Ibid., I, pr. 1, 5.

18. *Symp.* 31 (*Le Banquet*, p. 70).

19. Ibid., 92 (*Le Banquet*, p. 126).

20. Ibid., 284 (*Le Banquet*, p. 310).

21. Ibid., 293 (*Le Banquet*, p. 323).

22. *Bulletin of the Institute of Classical Studies* 18 (1971), 65.

23. *Laurentius von Durham* (cit. chap. I, n. 3), p. 60.

24. *De nuptiis* 911–919.

25. Ibid., 806–808.

26. *Cons.* I, pr. 4, 1.

27. I have discussed this imagery of the egg more fully in *Fabula* (cit. n. 5), chap. II, "Fables of the Cosmic Egg", esp. pp. 81–83.

28. Aristophanes, *The Birds*, 694–699, tr. William Arrowsmith (Ann Arbor, 1961), pp. 50–51.

29. *Études sur le poème allégorique en France au Moyen Âge* (Berne, 1972), p. 27.

30. Ibid., pp. 22, 26.

31. See especially Proverbs 8, Wisdom 7, 22–8, 16, and Ecclesiasticus 24; on later uses of the Sapiential tradition, I have some observations in *Medieval Latin and the Rise of European Love-Lyric*, 2nd ed. (Oxford, 1968), I, 87–97; see also Marina Warner, *Monuments and Maidens* (London, 1985), chap. IX.

32. Hermas, *Pastor,* Vis. I, ii, 2; III, xiii, 1.

33. Parmenides, Fragments 1, 22–32; 2; 6, in Hermann Diels, Walther Kranz, *Die Fragmente der Vorsokratiker,* 6th ed. (Berlin, 1951), I, 230–233. On the difficult question, how much of Parmenides' poem might still have been accessible to Boethius in the early sixth century, see my observations in *Boethius,* ed. Manfred Fuhrmann, Joachim Gruber (Darmstadt, 1984), pp. 437–438.

34. *Fugitivi* 3–5, 12–21.

35. Fulgentius, *Mitologiae* I, 25 (*Opera,* ed. Rudolf Helm, Leipzig, 1898, pp. 13–14). The parallel was first noted by Pierre Courcelle, *La Consolation de Philosophie dans la tradition littéraire* (Paris, 1967), p. 20. It is highly probable, even if not wholly certain, that the *Mitologiae* was written before the *Consolatio:* on the likely date of the mythographer (end of the fifth century), see *Der Kleine Pauly,* II, 628.

36. *Cons.* I, pr. 1, 10.

37. "Philosophisches und Medizinisches in der 'Consolatio Philosophiae' des Boethius", in *Römische Philosophie,* ed. Gregor Maurach (Darmstadt, 1976), pp. 341–384.

38. *Cons.* I, pr. 2, 4–6.

39. Peter Abelard, *Expositio in Hexaemeron, Patrologia Latina* 178, 760 C.

40. V. L. Dedeck-Héry, ed., "Boethius' *De Consolatione* by Jean de Meun", *Mediaeval Studies* 14 (1952), 165–275, at p. 171. It is the merit of Roberto Crespo to have seen that Jean de Meun's preface to his translation of Boethius is closely similar to the preface of William of Aragon's *commentary* on the *Consolatio:* cf. "Il prologo alla traduzione della 'Consolatio Philosophiae' di Jean de Meun e il commento di Guglielmo d'Aragona", in *Romanitas et Christianitas. Studia Iano Henrico Waszink . . . oblata* (Amsterdam-London, 1973), pp. 55–70. I am not, however, convinced by Crespo's claim that William of Aragon's preface is prior to Jean's. There is a *prima facie* problem in that the explicit of the Erfurt MS containing William's commentary bears the date 1335, whereas Jean de Meun completed his translation in 1298 and died in 1305. But according to Crespo "la data contenuta in un explicit non sarà certo sufficiente a revocar in dubbio la quasi ovvia direzione del rapporto" (p. 60). He then adduces two passages which to him "paiono render improbabile una traduzione dal francese in latino" (p. 61). In my view, these passages offer no evidence concerning priority: they show only the difference between a spirited and inventive writer of French and a rather more conventional writer of Latin, and I fail to see how the direction of the debt can be inferred from them, let alone be called "quasi ovvia". While it is relatively unusual among learned works for a Latin-writing author to imitate a vernacular one, this is by no means improbable if the vernacular author was as renowned, and as far-reachingly original in thought, as Jean de Meun. Even if we grant that the date "1335" in the Erfurt MS refers to the completion of the copy, not

of William's commentary itself, the little we know about his career suggests
that he was a younger—not an older—contemporary of Jean de Meun's:
see especially Marcel Thomas, "Guillaume d'Aragon, Auteur du *Liber de
nobilitate animi*", *Bibliothèque de l'Ecole des Chartes* 106 (1945–1946), 70–79,
at p. 75.

41. "How to Read the *Consolation of Philosophy*", *Interpretation* 14
(1986), 211–263 (the passage cited here is on pp. 244–246); and "The Consolation of Philosophy as a Work of Literature", *American Journal of Philology*
108 (1987), 343–367. Particularly valuable also is Joachim Gruber's *Kommentar zu Boethius De Consolatione Philosophiae* (Berlin-New York, 1978):
see esp. the section "Die literarische Tradition in der Consolatio
Philosophiae", pp. 16–35. Notwithstanding its promising title, Caroline D.
Eckhardt's essay, "The Medieval *Prosimetrum* Genre (from Boethius to
Boece)", *Genre* 16 (1983), 21–38, should be used with extreme caution: the
author shows disconcerting lapses in chronology (e.g. "Menippus' own
choice of mixed prose and verse may have been influenced by the Arabic
maqama, a prosimetric humorous discourse", p. 23), and lapses in the com-
mand of Latin (e.g. "metrical as in Virgil, rhythmical as in Primatis",
p. 22—the genitive of "Primas" has gone unrecognised).

42. *Cons.* I, m. 7, 1–13.

43. *Cons.* II, pr. 8, 2.

44. *Cons.* II, m. 8, 1–4, 13–21, 28–30. I have discussed the significance
and literary context of this poem more fully in the essay "L'amor che move
il sole e l'altre stelle" (1965, repr. with some revisions in my *The Medieval
Poet and his World*, Rome, 1984, pp. 439–475).

45. See especially R. B. C. Huygens, "Mittelalterliche Kommentare
zum 'O qui perpetua'", *Sacris Erudiri* 6 (1954), 373–426; Dronke, *Fabula*
(cit. n. 5), pp. 85–88, 157–158.

46. Gruber, *Kommentar*, pp. 277–290; the older discussion in Friedrich
Klingner, *De Boethii Consolatione Philosophiae* (Berlin, 1921), pp. 38–67,
also remains valuable.

47. *Cons.* III, m. 9, 22–28.

48. *Cons.* III, m. 9, 6.

49. *Cons.* IV, m. 4, 12.

50. See above, p. 6.

51. Hildebert, *Liber de querimonia et conflictu carnis et spiritus seu animae*,
Patrologia Latina 171, 989–1004 (but see also n. 53 below); Adelard, *De
eodem et diverso*, ed. Hans Willner, *Beiträge zur Geschichte der Philosophie des
Mittelalters* IV, 1 (1903); Bernardus Silvestris, *Cosmographia*, ed. Peter
Dronke (Leiden, 1978); Alan, *De planctu Naturae*, ed. N. M. Häring, *Studi
medievali*, ser. 3, 19 (1978), 797–879.

52. Cf. *Cosmographia*, pp. 7–10, and the *Erratum* to p. 10, l. 16.

53. The fullest list to date of manuscripts of Hildebert's *prosimetrum* is
that included with manuscripts of his letters in Peter von Moos, *Hildebert*

von Lavardin (Stuttgart, 1965), pp. 360–365, under "Quer<imonia>". To these should be added London B.L. Add. 24199 (s. XII ex.), and Paris B.N. lat. 2908 (s. XIII, which I have used for the citations below). Von Moos has a perceptive discussion of the work, ibid., pp. 118–130.

54. I cite the opening from Paris B.N. lat. 2908, fol. 1r-v. This seems to me to offer a slightly better text than B.N. lat. 14867 (s. XII²), fol. 1r, and a considerably better one than *Patrologia Latina* 171, 989–990. Only the last word cited, *mei,* is miswritten *mee* in lat. 2908.

55. There would seem to be an implicit allegory here of the soul, or inner being, sullied by original sin and needing the water of baptism to wash its stains away. I am indebted to Ursula Dronke for this observation.

56. *Epist.* I, 6, 12.

57. B.N. lat. 2908, fol. 3r (B.N. lat. 14867, fol. 3r; *P.L.* 171, 992 C).

58. The text should read *diuturnarum libertatem feriarum* (MSS), and not *diurnarum libertatem fenarium* (*P.L.* 171, 993 A).

59. B.N. lat. 2908, fol. 4v (B.N. lat. 14867, fol. 4v; *P.L.* 171, 994 B).

60. *Cons.* I, m. 2, 1–3.

61. B.N. lat. 2908, fol. 5r (B.N. lat. 14867, fol. 4v; *P.L.* 171, 994 B).

62. Cf. *De quantitate animae,* II, xxxiii, 70–76; Hildebert names them: *vivificatio, sensus, ars, correctio, virtus, contemplatio, quies.*

63. B.N. lat. 14867, fol. 12v (B.N. lat. 2908, fol. 12v, reading *dum declamat eamque; P.L.* 171, 1004 A).

64. The two versions of the Anglo-Saxon "Soul and Body" are printed in *The Anglo-Saxon Poetic Records,* ed. G. P. Krapp, E. V. K. Dobbie, II (New York, 1932), 54–59, and III (New York, 1936), 174–178. Cf. also M. J. B. Allen, D. G. Calder, *Sources and Analogues of Old English Poetry* (Cambridge-Totowa, 1976), pp. 40–50; and, for the later texts, Hans Walther, *Das Streitgedicht in der lateinischen Literatur des Mittelalters* (2nd ed., rev. P. G. Schmidt, Hildesheim-Zurich-New York, 1984), pp. 62–81, 262–263 (including some valuable references relating to vernacular versions).

III Narrative and the Mixed Form

1. Ed. Ulrich von Wilamowitz-Moellendorf, *Vitae Homeri et Hesiodi* (Bonn, 1916), pp. 3–21. Numbers below refer to sections in this edition.

2. There is an attractive adaptation by Wolfgang Schadewaldt, *Legende von Homer dem fahrenden Sänger* (Leipzig, 1942); unfortunately, the words "übersetzt und erläutert", on the title-page, give a misleading impression of the book's content. Schadewaldt, though using the text in Wilamowitz, treated this with considerable freedom, inserting substantial extracts from the *Certamen* in the midst of the *Vita* (*Legende* pp. 35–45), and elsewhere abridging, readjusting, summarising, and cutting. He signals some of these procedures at *Legende* p. 96, n. 10; others—such as the complete omission of *Vita* 37–38—receive no mention.

3. *Hesiod, The Homeric Hymns and Homerica,* ed. and tr. H. G. Evelyn-White (rev. ed., Cambridge, Mass., 1936), pp. 566–597, 624–627. In the discussion below, I cite the text of the *Certamen* from Wilamowitz, *Vitae,* pp. 34–45.

4. Fragment 56, in Diels-Kranz, *Fragmente* (cit. chap. II, n. 33), I, 163.

5. Athenaeus, *Deipnosophistae,* VIII, 360. On the genre and its functions, see Michael Herzfeld, "Ritual and Textual Structures", in *Text and Context. The Social Anthropology of Tradition,* ed. R. K. Jain (Philadelphia, 1977), pp. 29–50.

6. See especially the perceptive and wide-ranging study by Reinhold Merkelbach, "Bettelgedichte", *Rheinisches Museum,* N. F. 95 (1952), 312–327; to this I also owe my knowledge of the Vedic hymn cited below.

7. *Der Rig-Veda,* tr. K. F. Geldner (Cambridge, Mass.-London-Leipzig, 1951), I, 173–174. My translation here is based primarily on Geldner's German, but I am deeply grateful to Gregory Nagy for advice about the nuances in the original.

8. Once, in the *Certamen* (Wilamowitz, p. 43), the narrator says explicitly of Homer: "he is said to have improvised these verses" (σχεδιάσαι λέγεται τούσδε τοὺς στίχους).

9. *Eddadigte II: Gudedigte,* ed. Jón Helgason (Copenhagen-Oslo-Stockholm, 1956), pp. 1–10.

10. *Certamen,* p. 38.

11. *Vita,* 34; cf. *Certamen,* p. 44.

12. *Certamen,* p. 36.

13. See above, n. 4.

14. This is not, however, the point that Heraclitus makes: he sees the episode as an illustration of the fact that even the wisest of men can be "deceived in the knowledge of visible things".

15. *Liadain and Curithir,* ed. and tr. Kuno Meyer (London, 1902), p. 9. (I retain Meyer's spellings of names in the discussion below.) More recently, Gerard Murphy, *Early Irish Lyrics* (Oxford, 1956), p. 82, has dated Liadain's lament to ca. 875.

16. Charles Plummer, *Vitae Sanctorum Hiberniae* (Oxford, 1910), I, lxxix.

17. Meyer, *Liadain,* p. 8. Cf. Murphy, *Lyrics,* p. 211.

18. On the various possible relations between poetry and its prose context or frame in early Irish, see esp. the recent study by Proinsias Mac Cana, "Notes on the Combination of Prose and Verse in Early Irish Narrative", in *Early Irish Literature/Mündlichkeit und Schriftlichkeit,* ed. S. N. Tranter, H. C. L. Tristram (Tübingen, 1989), pp. 125–147. Mac Cana does not, however, discuss *Liadain and Curithir* itself. For arguments in favour of the existence of narratives in the mixed form in medieval Welsh and Old English, see most recently Nicolas Jacobs, "Celtic Saga and the Contexts of Old English Elegiac Poetry", *Études Celtiques* 26 (1989), 95–142.

19. Meyer, *Liadain*, pp. 16–17.

20. On the background of this motif, cf. Louis Gougaud, "*Mulierum consortia:* Étude sur le syneisaktisme chez les ascètes celtiques", *Ériu* 9 (1921–1923), 147–156.

21. I have cited the verses above from Murphy, *Lyrics,* pp. 82–84, except that, for the third verse, I adopt the reading and suggested rendering of Anders Ahlqvist, "A Line in *Líadan and Cuirithir*", *Peritia* 1 (1982), 334. Otherwise I have taken Murphy and Meyer as my guides for translation, with the exception of the verse *is fírithir ad-fíadar,* where I follow the suggestion of Wolfgang Meid (ed.), *Beiträge zur Indogermanistik und Keltologie, Julius Pokorny zum 80. Geburtstag gewidmet* (Innsbruck, 1967), pp. 235–236. Other English translations, with some differences of emphasis, are to be found (along with the text) in James Carney, *Medieval Irish Lyrics* (Dublin, 1967), pp. 24–29, and David Greene, Frank O'Connor, *A Golden Treasury of Irish Poetry* (London, 1967), pp. 72–74. I am grateful to Patrick Sims-Williams for the references to Ahlqvist and Meid, and for advice and help on a number of points of meaning.

22. This is what the narrator suggests in the prose coda (Meyer, *Liadain,* pp. 26–27).

23. *Kormáks Saga,* ed. Einar Ólafur Sveinsson, *Íslenzk Fornrit* VIII (Reykjavík, 1939), 201–302.

24. *The Genesis of a Saga Narrative. Verse and Prose in Kormaks Saga* (Oxford, 1991). Cf. also Einar Ólafur Sveinsson, "Kormakr the Poet and his Verses", *Saga-Book of the Viking Society* 18/1 (1966), 18–60; Hans Schottmann, "Der Bau der *Kormaks Saga*", *Skandinavistik* 12 (1982), 22–36.

25. "Kormakr the Poet", p. 37.

26. *The Genesis,* p. 22.

27. "Hlín" was an ancient poetic name for the goddess Frigg; Snorri, in the early thirteenth century, explains its meaning as "bringing peace or wellbeing", but was probably just guessing: see Jan de Vries, *Altgermanische Religionsgeschichte,* 2nd ed. (Berlin, 1957), II, 327.

28. *The Genesis,* pp. 110, 156.

29. Cf. ibid., pp. 160, 174–175.

30. Ibid., pp. 175, 177.

31. It is significant that such prose elaborations scarcely exist for lyrics of troubadours who composed before 1150, however illustrious they were as poets.

32. Uc de San Circ, writing of the troubadour Savaric de Malleo: *Le biografie trovadoriche,* ed. Guido Favati (Bologna, 1961), p. 311; *Biographies des troubadours,* ed. Jean Boutière, A. H. Schutz, tr. I.-M. Cluzel, 2nd ed. (Paris, 1973), p. 224.

33. E.g. by Helga Reuschel, "Gedichtreihen und Dichterleben in der isländischen Saga", *Wirkendes Wort* 11 (1961), 266–271; Bjarni Einarsson, *To skjaldesagaer* (Bergen-Oslo-Tromsø, 1976), pp. 15–16.

34. For the single exception—the expanded version of Guillem de Cabestanh's life, which runs to nearly six pages—see Favati, pp. 203–208, Boutière-Schutz-Cluzel, pp. 544–549.

35. The statistics are slightly approximate, since editors do not always agree whether a text is a variant of another *razo* or a piece in its own right. Favati's edition counts 61 *razos*, only one of which (for Lanfranc Cigala) is later than Uc de San Circ. I have based figures on Favati; those of Boutière-Schutz-Cluzel differ only in minor respects.

36. Cf. Favati, *Biografie,* p. 105, n. 178. Occasionally, among the texts that we can plausibly ascribe to Uc, there is a hint of concatenation—a cross-reference, of the kind "You have already heard . . .", to another *razo* or to a *vida*. In these somewhat rare cases we can read up to about five pages as if they formed a continuous biographical account with illustrative verses—yet clearly in scope this is still a far cry from the Icelandic poets' sagas.

37. Favati, pp. 265–271; Boutière-Schutz-Cluzel, pp. 351–354. Here the *vida* and the first *razo* show "concatenation" of the kind described in n. 36.

38. The strophe is cited in Boutière-Schutz-Cluzel, p. 354; for a complete ed. and tr. of the poem, with commentary, see *Les poésies du Moine de Montaudon,* ed. M. J. Routledge (Montpellier, 1977), pp. 153–170.

39. *Peire Vidal, Poesie,* ed. D'Arco Silvio Avalle (2 vols., Milan-Naples, 1960), I, 7–8.

40. Avalle, *Peire* v, 34; x, 10; xv, 20; xvii, 30; xviii, 19; xxxiv, 23 (*emperi*).

41. See Peire's *tenso* with Manfredi Lancia, ibid., xliv.

42. Ibid., v, 33–34.

43. Ibid., v, 41–44.

44. Favati, p. 270; Boutière-Schutz-Cluzel, pp. 368–369. Cf. Ezra Pound, "Peire Vidal Old," in his *Personae* (London, 1952), pp. 44–46.

As Michael Reeve has reminded me, there is a curious ancient analogue to this episode in Longus' *Daphnis and Chloe,* I, 20–22, in the misadventure of Chloe's wooer Dorcon, who disguises himself in a wolfskin in order to steal close to his beloved. But, Peire Vidal's alleged Greek links notwithstanding, a direct connection with the poem or the *razo* seems unlikely.

45. Favati, pp. 266–269 (two versions); Boutière-Schutz-Cluzel, pp. 356–358, 361–363.

46. *Kormáks Saga,* pp. 291–293, st. 76.

47. There is no single comprehensive guide to the labyrinth of versions of the *Romance.* For the ancient tradition, Reinhold Merkelbach, *Die Quellen des griechischen Alexanderromans,* 2nd ed. (Munich, 1977), is indispensable; for the Latin versions and their medieval vernacular derivatives,

see esp. D. J. A. Ross, *Alexander Historiatus* (London, 1963), and George Cary, *The Medieval Alexander* (Cambridge, 1956). For what follows I have used principally *Historia Alexandri Magni, I, Recensio Vetusta,* ed. Wilhelm Kroll (Berlin, 1926).

48. This hymn survives only in the so-called Γ-recension of the *Romance: Der griechische Alexanderroman, Rezension Γ, Buch I,* ed. Ursula von Lauenstein (Meisenheim, 1962), pp. 54–56.

49. *Historia,* ed. Kroll, pp. 55–59 (vv. 1–3, 16–22, 81–83). The verses, which are corrupt and fragmentary in several places, were composed ca. 300 A.D. They are iambic and choliambic trimeters, with many resolutions of the *longa;* they are "unclassical" in their predominant stress on the penultimate syllable, but this feature can already be found in Babrius' *Fables* (probably second century A.D.). I am indebted to Reinhold Merkelbach for advice on this point.

50. These verses again survive in the Γ-recension, *Buch III,* ed. Franz Parthe (Meisenheim, 1969), p. 450.

51. *Iuli Valerii res gestae Alexandri Macedonis,* ed. Bernard Kuebler (Leipzig, 1888). Julius Valerius was consul in 338 A.D.; this allows an approximate indication of date for the Latin text. The lyrical plea of the flautist (unnamed in the Latin), which occupies 83 verses in the *Recensio Vetusta,* is reduced to 31 verses in Julius' free rendering. It is noteworthy, however, that Julius follows his verses by a phrase which has no equivalent in the Greek text:

Addebat et fabulas, quaecumque Thebanae sunt, et memorias religiosas, quas vetus historia commendat. (p. 63, 31–33)

The wording used to describe these Theban legends and these religious narratives handed down in stories of old seems to distinguish their mode of presentation from that of the preceding verses, which were described as "singing the most artistic song he could devise" (*melos, quam posset fabrile, canere,* p. 62, 25). This suggests to me that Julius imagined the flautist presenting his pleas to Alexander in the form of a *prosimetrum,* the song being followed by prose recitatives. Between lines 12 and 13 of his verses, Julius likewise inserts *Addebat etiam* ("he also added"). Such an incision in the midst of the poetic imprecations is quite unexpected, and again has no equivalent in the Greek: could it perhaps indicate that the two lyrical passages (1–12, 14–31) were thought of as bridged by a flute solo?

52. *Iuli Valerii Epitome* (ca. ninth century A.D.), ed. Julius Zacher (Leipzig, 1867).

53. The manuscript tradition has been meticulously analysed by G. A. A. Kortekaas, *Historia Apollonii Regis Tyri* (Groningen, 1984), who offers a magisterial critical ed. of the two main versions of *Apollonius* (generally

known as RA and RB). There is also an excellent recent study of the story, by Elizabeth Archibald: *Apollonius of Tyre. Medieval and Renaissance Themes and Variations* (Woodbridge, 1991). This includes a text of RA, based on Kortekaas, with facing English translation.

54. It is defective preservation, rather than intrinsic flaws of narrative structure, that underlies at least some of the seeming illogicalities in the plot of *Apollonius*. Thus for instance, in *The Ancient Romances* (Berkeley–Los Angeles, 1967), Ben Edwin Perry objected (p. 298), when Apollonius guesses the incestuous king's riddle but is allowed a month's grace to go free:

> Would the crafty Antiochus turn about and become so stupid as to suppose that Apollonius would ever return to Antioch of his own accord, when he knew very well that if he did so he would be killed? . . . Obviously Antiochus could not have acted so foolishly under the circumstances given us. Why, then, is he represented as doing so? . . . We must conclude that the Latin author introduced this self-defeating action on the part of Antiochus for no other purpose than to motivate the travels and adventures of Apollonius in exile, disregarding . . . the requirements of the context into which he has brought it.

However, if one looks a little further than the Latin prose transmission, I think the original logic and coherence of this episode become clear. In the mid-twelfth-century Old French poetic fragment (ed. Alfred Schulze, *Zeitschrift für romanische Philologie* 33 [1909], 226–229; for the dating, cf. Maurice Delbouille, *Mélanges Rita Lejeune* II [Gembloux, 1969], 1176), we read:

> La pucele poor avoit,
> D'Appollonie molt se cremo<it>,
> Les deus prioit secree<ment>
> Que le roi müent sun <talent>,
> Que il Apollonie n'ocie;
> Poise li qu'or l'a en bal<lie>.
> La cors le roi ert molt <pleniere>
> Por la dame qu'avoi<ent chiere>;
> Tuit erent venu escol<ter>
> Apollonie öir deviner.
> N'i a celui deu ne proia<st>
> Qu'Apollonies adevinas<t>. (3–14)

The girl was afraid—she was very anxious about Apollonius, she secretly prayed to the gods that they change the king's intent of killing him: it weighs on her that he now has Apollonius in his power. The king's court was very full, because of the lady, whom they held dear. All had come to listen, to hear Apollonius make his guess, nor was there any among them who did not beseech God that Apollonius would solve the riddle.

That is, Antiochus was not alone when Apollonius gave his answer, as the Latin prose versions (chap. 6), where the king goes on to summon his steward Taliarchus, suggest. In the version known to the Old French poet, Antiochus' people were not only present at the ordeal but were hoping, like the princess, that Apollonius would triumph. They heard his solution of the riddle—"Sire, your daughter is your mistress" (30)—and saw the signs of guilt in the king's looks: "he became pale with anger, one moment he was white, the next he grew red, he cut short his words, because of his people, who were beginning to notice" (35–38). In other words, Antiochus could not have executed Apollonius at that moment without jeopardising his own reign. So he is forced to play for time: "'Friend', he said, 'it is not so. I shall let you go without killing you'" (39–40, the last complete verses legible in the fragment). That such a version of the events existed from early times can likewise be inferred from certain details in the tenth-century Latin verse fragment, *Gesta Apollonii* (ed. Ernst Dümmler, *Poetae Latini Aevi Carolini,* II, 483–506): there, when Apollonius enters "the tyrant's hall", respendent in golden robes like another Phoebus, the people of Antioch marvel at him, awestruck, "as if he were Jove come down from Olympus on high" (p. 491). This contrast between the tyrant and his god-like visitor, who worsts him before his subjects, helps to account for another detail in the Latin prose versions, which to Perry (*Romances,* p. 309) seemed "an unexplained mystery"—namely, that after Antiochus' death Apollonius should be offered the kingdom of Antioch (chap. 24).

55. Archibald, *Apollonius,* pp. 182–233, gives a valuable conspectus of "Latin and Vernacular Versions of *Historia Apollonii* to 1609" (the date of the First Quarto of Shakespeare's *Pericles*). For an account of some versions later than Shakespeare, I would signal especially R. M. Dawkins' delightful article, "Modern Greek Oral Versions of Apollonios of Tyre", *Modern Language Review* 37 (1942), 169–184.

56. *Bulletin of the Institute of Classical Studies* 18 (1971), 65.

57. For a text and discussion of the fragments, see esp. Mario Mazza, "Le avventure del romanzo nell'occidente latino. La *Historia Apollonii Regis Tyri*", in *Le trasformazioni della cultura nella tarda antichità,* ed. Claudia Giuffrida, Mario Mazza (Rome, 1985), II, 597–645, at pp. 610–615. The rela-

tion of the narrative content of the Greek fragments to that of the Latin *Apollonius* is problematic, yet, as Mazza suggests, this could well be the counterpart to Archestrates' daughter's love for Apollonius (chaps. 15–20)—shown in an openly erotic way in the Greek, but with timid, decorous indirectness in the Latin. The occurrence of the name "Apollonios" in both Greek fragments makes it very unlikely, in my view, that these should belong to an entirely different story, as some scholars have suggested.

58. *Apollonius,* chap. 11.

59. The Vergilian and Ovidian echoes are listed by Kortekaas, *ad loc.,* pp. 298–300; they concern five of the sixteen verses: 3–4, 10, 16–17 (in Kortekaas' line-numbering, 10–11, 17, 23–24); a sixth (Kortekaas 22) is modelled on a verse of Silius Italicus.

60. I have discussed this concept in the essay "Medieval Rhetoric" (1965, repr. with some revisions in my *The Medieval Poet and his World,* Rome, 1984, pp. 7–38), esp. pp. 24–27.

61. *Apollonius,* chap. 11; cf. *Aen.* 3, 69.

62. Ibid., chap. 41.

63. The author has chosen for his ten riddles *Aenigmata* 12, 2, 13, 90, 61, 63, 59, 69, 79, 78. In 90 (the riddle of the baths), as Kortekaas well notes (p. 382), Tarsia changes the wording of the second verse (from *est calor in medio magnus quem nemo veretur* to *circumdata flammis, hinc inde vallata, nec uror*), in such a way that it can be understood also of herself.

64. In T. S. Eliot's variation on the Apollonius story, "Marina" (*Collected Poems 1909–1935,* London, 1936, pp. 113–114), the father has the lines "What images return / O my daughter."

65. *Apollonius,* chap. 42.

66. I suspect the original sequence of the riddles in the *Apollonius* has been lost in this one instance—that in chap. 42 the fourth riddle, that of the baths (Kortekaas, p. 382, Archibald, p. 164, 27–29), should come as the sixth, at the close of this chapter, immediately before the seventh riddle, that of the ball, which opens chap. 43. In this way the baths and the ball, which belonged together in the narrative (chap. 13), would remain together in the series of riddles.

67. Not long after writing the above suggestions about the symbolic meaning of Tarsia's riddles, I was able to see Michel Zink's *Le roman d'Apollonius de Tyr* (Paris, 1982), an edition and translation of a fourteenth-century French prose version of the romance. In his introduction (pp. 26–36), Zink gives an ingenious and stimulating interpretation of these riddles. I am not wholly convinced by all his conjectures (e.g. about the sexual connotations of the ball and the sponge, or the solar ones of the chariot). As these would require, and deserve, a fuller discussion than is possible in the present context, I have left my own—more minimal—

interpretations unaltered. Whatever divergences may remain in the detailed reading of the riddles, I feel as certain as Zink that they were weighted symbolically and that none was chosen randomly.

68. An outstanding example in Latin, in my opinion, is the story of the doomed love of Hagbard and Signe, as it is presented by Saxo Grammaticus, *Gesta Danorum,* VII, vii. Here, however fecund the oral tradition that Saxo inherited and utilised may have been, I believe we can also say that it is he, in his exceptional literary virtuosity, who is responsible for the fully achieved prosimetric tale. On Saxo's artistry, and his relation to the Latin prosimetric tradition, see esp. Karsten Friis-Jensen, *Saxo* (cit. chap. I, n. 3).

69. Jean Dufournet, in *Aucassin et Nicolette, Édition critique,* 2nd ed. (Paris, 1984), which is cited below, leaves the question open: "soit dans le dernier quart du XIIe siècle, soit dans la première moitié du XIIIe siècle" (p. 3). For a suggestion that would lead to a later dating, ca. 1270, see Brian Blakey, *French Studies* 22 (1968), 97–98. The secondary literature on *Aucassin et Nicolette* is immense: see esp. B. N. Sargent-Baur, R. F. Cook, *Aucassin et Nicolette: A Critical Bibliography* (London, 1981). Among recent studies, I have found of particular interest Tony Hunt, "La parodie médiévale: le cas d'*Aucassin et Nicolette*", *Romania* 100 (1979), 341–381, and Charles Méla, "C'est d'Aucassin et Nicolette", in his *Blanchefleur et le saint homme* (Paris, 1979), pp. 47–73.

70. "Sur les pièces lyriques du *Tristan* en prose", *Mélanges Félix Lecoy* (Paris, 1973), pp. 19–25, at p. 20.

71. The prose *Tristan* was composed in the 1230s; on the date of the Vienna MS, see *Le roman de Tristan en prose,* I, ed. Philippe Ménard (Geneva, 1987), pp. 10–11. This volume contains three of the *lais:* pp. 230 (Kahedin), 233–234 (Yseut), 238–242 (Kahedin).

72. Tatiana Fotitch, Ruth Steiner, *Les lais du roman de Tristan en prose d'après le manuscrit de Vienne 2542* (Munich, 1974). Fotitch and Steiner, however, like other earlier scholars, dated this MS erroneously to the "troisième quart du XVe siècle" (p. 14).

73. See Peter Dronke, Michael Lapidge, Peter Stotz, "Die unveröffentlichten Gedichte der Cambridge Liederhandschrift", *Mittellateinisches Jahrbuch* 17 (1982), 54–95, at pp. 94–95; M. T. Gibson, Michael Lapidge, Christopher Page, "Neumed Boethian *metra* from Canterbury", *Anglo-Saxon England* 12 (1983), 140–152.

74. Cf. Dufournet, *Aucassin,* p. 165, citing Mario Roques.

75. There are, however, certain parallels to this in Latin in the *Cosmographia* of Bernardus Silvestris: see above, p. 46.

76. *Aucassin* VI (Dufournet, p. 58).

77. Cf. Gustave Cohen, "Une curieuse et vieille coutume folklorique: la 'Couvade'", *Studi medievali,* N.S. 17 (1951), 114–123.

78. *Aucassin* XXX (Dufournet, p. 134).

79. Juan Ruiz, *Libro de Buen Amor*, sts. 1067–1127; cf. also the Italian play (first printed in 1552, but with older medieval roots), *La guerra di Carnevale e Quaresima,* ed. Vincenzo De Bartholomaeis, *Laude drammatiche e rappresentazioni sacre,* III (Florence, 1943), 165–185.

80. *Aucassin* XXXII (Dufournet, p. 138).

81. Ibid., XXIV (Dufournet, pp. 114, 118).

82. *Aucassin* XVIII (Dufournet, pp. 96–98). The motif of excessive valuation of the beloved has a parallel in Kormakr's verses: he values one eye of Steingerðr's "at three hundreds", and her hair "at five hundreds" (st. 7, *Kormáks Saga,* pp. 212–213); he then values her person "at the whole of Iceland, as far as farthest Hunland, and Denmark too; she is worth the ground of England and of Ireland . . ." (st. 8, ibid.).

83. On the motif of the love-chase, in which the beloved is the quarry to be pursued, see Marcelle Thiébaux, *The Stag of Love* (Ithaca-London, 1974), esp. chap. III.

84. When the lovers find each other again in the forest, Nicolette also heals Aucassin physically, setting his dislocated shoulder—but significantly, she does this "according to the will of God, who loves lovers" (*Aucassin* XXVI, Dufournet, p. 124).

85. Ibid., XI, 16–28 (Dufournet, pp. 74–76)..

86. The question of the extent to which *Aucassin et Nicolette* is rooted in a popular tradition of storytelling—even if, in its extant form, it is a consummately designed work of literary art—remains difficult. One relevant *donnée,* not so far as I know considered before, is the tale *Étoilette,* which was published by Henriette-Julie de Castelnau, Comtesse de Murat, in her *Les Lutins du château de Kernosy* (Paris, 1710). (I owe my knowledge of this work to the kindness of Marina Warner). *Étoilette,* entirely in prose, is sufficiently close to *Aucassin et Nicolette* in all essentials—including a topsy-turvy kingdom called "l'isle du Repos", where the King rests but the Queen and the women fight a carnivalised combat—for one to be sure that its resemblances to the medieval text cannot be fortuitous. Yet there are also sufficient points of difference in the plot (quite apart from various accretions that belong to the *koinê* of fairy-tale) for it to be improbable that Madame de Murat was going back directly to the Old French. It is intrinsically unlikely that she had consulted the unique known manuscript, in what was then the Bibliothèque Royale, and there was no printed version available when she wrote: La Curne de Sainte-Palaye's translation into modern French was first published in the *Mercure de France* in February 1752, the original not till 1808. Yet it seems to me likely that the medieval *Aucassin et Nicolette* existed in further MSS and gave rise to various oral retellings in the later Middle Ages, retellings that could have circulated in

oral and perhaps also written forms till the early eighteenth century (in *Les Lutins, Étoilette* is allegedly read out from a handwritten composition by a member of the assembled company). The other possibility—that the medieval literary text and *Étoilette* should be two entirely independent witnesses to a more archaic oral tradition—while it cannot be totally excluded, seems much less probable. (See also p. 143.)

87. *Aucassin* I, 10–15 (Dufournet, p. 42). Note especially the precise verbal echo—*entrepris, / de grant mal amaladis*—that links the two lyrical passages, I and XI.

IV   The Poetic and the Empirical "I"

1. *Women Writers of the Middle Ages: A Critical Study of Texts from Perpetua († 203) to Marguerite Porete († 1310)* (Cambridge, 1984), chaps. II and VII. The fourth impression (1988) incorporates some corrections and two pages of Addenda (pp. 332–333).

2. "Note on the Poetic and the Empirical 'I' in Medieval Authors", cit. chap. I, n. 4.

3. Ibid., p. 104.

4. Ibid., pp. 102–103.

5. *Liber manualis;* I have used the ed. of Pierre Riché, *Dhuoda, Manuel pour mon fils,* with tr. by Bernard de Vregille and Claude Mondésert (Paris, 1975). For the passages cited below, however, I have also compared the MS Barcelona, Biblioteca Central 569.

6. Smaragdus: *Patrologia Latina* 102, 933–970; Jonas of Orléans: ed. Jean Reviron (Paris, 1930). On the genre up to and including the Carolingian period, see esp. Pierre Hadot, "Fürstenspiegel"; *Reallexikon für Antike und Christentum* VIII (1972), 555–632, who does not, however, mention Dhuoda.

Wilhelm Meyer (*Nachrichten der Göttingen Akad. der Wiss.,* 1907, pp. 39–74) edited a brief prose *Monitum* (pp. 55–60), and some verse advice to a *rex* (pp. 61–69), which he was inclined to see as one composite work, in prose and verse, again by Smaragdus, composed between 817 and 821. More recently this was qualified by H. H. Anton, *Fürstenspiegel und Herrscherethos in der Karolingerzeit* (Bonn, 1968), who pointed out (p. 186) that the prose *Monitum* (which in fact is attributed to Alcuin in the unique MS) was a slightly reworked version of a Merovingian letter to a king. According to Franz Brunhölzl, *Geschichte der lateinischen Literatur des Mittelalters,* I (Munich, 1975), 447–448, a relation between the prose and verse pieces is not certain, and neither piece is likely to be by Smaragdus. Thus the question, whether Dhuoda might have known Meyer's prose and verse compositions in a single context (as they occur in his MS, London B.L.

Royal C. XXIII), and might have found a stimulus to her own large-scale *prosimetrum* in what appeared to be a small *opus geminatum,* is an intriguing one, but, in the present state of research, cannot pass beyond conjecture.

7. Ed. Siegmund Hellmann, *Sedulius Scottus* (Munich, 1906), pp. 1–91.

8. *Manuel,* p. 68. I have corrected to *atque motibus:* the passage is extant only in the Barcelona MS, which has *moribus atque,* and in the seventeenth-century Paris MS (B.N. lat. 12293), which according to Riché has *motibus atque.*

9. Ibid., pp. 68–70.

10. Ibid., pp. 74–76.

11. The reading *indignam* in the Barcelona MS, not noted by Riché, can be accepted, construed in apposition to *similem* in the previous verse. I am assuming that Barcelona here preserves an "incorrectness" of Dhuoda's, and that *genitrixque sua* (*sum* understood) functions as a separate syntactic unit. On Dhuoda's uses of *mis,* see esp. Dag Norberg, *La poésie latine rythmique du haut moyen âge* (Stockholm, 1954), p. 16.

12. *Manuel,* pp. 80–82.

13. On the verses see esp. Heinz Antony, "Korruptel oder Lemma?", *Mittellateinisches Jahrbuch* 16 (1981), 288–333, at pp. 289–301, 332–333.

14. *Manuel,* pp. 182, 200, 228–230, 242–244, 252.

15. See above, chap. I, pp. 14–19.

16. *Manuel,* p. 340, 25.

17. *Manuel,* IX; Riché's division of the *Liber manualis* into sections— while it could be debated in certain details for other parts of the work—is clearly appropriate in the case of the three concluding sections, IX–XI.

18. Dhuoda's stress, however, does not always fall on a stem-syllable, as is the rule in Germanic verse.

19. *Manuel,* pp. 344–346.

20. The strophe is difficult. Riché's suggestion (p. 347, n. 1), "Nous supposons qu'il faut lire *gradatim*", in place of *gradans* in the MSS, belongs, I think, in the text: the scribe of the archetype will have been looking ahead to *peragrans. Peragrans* (*est* understood) appears to be used without object here; I take the subject to be *iuventus tua.* I do not think, with Riché and the translators, that *senioribus* can mean "prennent de l'âge": Dhuoda regularly uses *senior* and *seniores* to refer to lords in the feudal sense (cf. e.g. *Liber* III, 4, at 1, 2, 12, 18, 31, 37, and 43, *Manuel,* pp. 148–150), though she also uses *senior* to refer to God (*Deus et senior tuus, Liber* III, 4, 49, ibid.). I would construe *senioribus* here, literally, as "among lords". *Longior,* finally, at the opening of the next strophe, I construe as still having *iuventus* as subject, and hence do not place a full stop after *peragrans.*

21. Possibly the sense is "I who long to see how your handsome looks have developed" (literally, *tue speciei tenorem* could mean "the career of your beauty").

22. *Manuel,* p. 350. Cf. *Women Writers,* p. 53: "Here the words 'no one like you *(nullum similem tui)*' echo those in the opening verse epigraph: 'he will never have anyone like me *(Mis michi similem non habebit unquam)*'".

23. Ed. P. L. D. Reid, *Corpus Christianorum,* Cont. Med., XLIV A (1984), 197–218. The edition of the *Proemium* of *Phrenesis* in Fritz Weigle, *Die Briefe des Bischofs Rather von Verona (MGH,* Weimar, 1949), pp. 54–66, remains valuable, especially for its notes.

24. A third such débâcle at Verona was to happen late in Rather's life, in 965: see esp. Georg Misch, *Geschichte der Autobiographie* II, 2 (Frankfurt am Main, 1955), 625.

25. Cf. Weigle, *Briefe,* notes to pp. 61–62.

26. Reid, p. 203, 189; Weigle, p. 63, 13. The sentence is unfortunately corrupt in the *editio princeps* (by Pietro and Geronimo Ballerini, Verona, 1765, reproduced in *Patrologia Latina* 136), and no manuscript survives.

27. Misch, *Geschichte* II, 2, 519–650; Erich Auerbach, *Literatursprache und Publikum in der lateinischen Spätantike und im Mittelalter* (Berne, 1958), pp. 99–113.

28. Reid, p. 200, 44–51; Weigle, pp. 57, 14–58, 2.

29. Reid, p. 201, 87–90; Weigle, p. 59, 21–25.

30. Reid, p. 205, 267–268; Weigle, p. 66, 5–6.

31. Reid, p. 206, 283 *(omine forsitan neque penitus vano).*

32. Reid, p. 211, 494–503.

33. Reid, p. 213, 586–587.

34. Reid, p. 214, 598–599.

35. *P.L.* 136, 388 D: "Sententia certe valde obscura et difficilis est, ut vix in fine aliquid elicietur."

36. Reid, pp. 214–215, 630–633; the allusion to Isaiah is not identified either here or in the Ballerini edition.

37. Reid, pp. 215–216, 669–674. I have capitalised *Constantia* in 670: she is clearly conceived as a personification here.

38. Rather drew this name (and accusative form) from Juvenal 3, 266.

39. Reid, p. 217, 687–692. At 687 Reid (following the *ed. princ.*) prints *Lamas nec;* I owe the correction to Michael Reeve.

40. The work as we have it concludes with a prose invective addressing Rather's other enemy, *Baldricus invidus,* the Bishop of Utrecht, and with Rather's solemn formulaic profession of his own true religious faith (Reid, pp. 217–218, 727–768).

41. Mechthild von Magdeburg, *Das fliessende Licht der Gottheit,* ed. Hans Neumann, *Band I: Text, besorgt von Gisela Vollmann-Profe* (Munich-Zurich, 1990); Marguerite Porete, *Le mirouer des simples ames,* ed. Romana Guarnieri / *Margaretae Porete Speculum simplicium animarum,* ed. Paul Verdeyen (*Corpus Christianorum,* Cont. Med., LXIX, 1986); Dante Alighieri, *Vita Nuova,* ed. Domenico De Robertis (Milan-Naples, 1980).

For the passages from Marguerite Porete cited below, I have compared the unique MS of the French text: Chantilly, Condé F xiv 26.

42. She is often "Dame Amour" (e.g. *Mirouer* pp. 44, 99; 46, 124), "Amour . . . maitresse" (p. 46, 141); nonetheless, when the person of Christ is uppermost in Marguerite's thought, she also at times addresses Amour as "sire" (e.g. p. 46, 130).

43. *V.N.* III, 3 *(una figura d'uno segnore di pauroso aspetto); XII, 3 (uno giovane vestito di bianchissime vestimenta).* De Robertis notes the *iuvenem . . . coopertum stola candida* of Mark 16, 5 and the *vir . . . in veste candida* of Acts 10, 30; but compare also 2 Maccabees 3, 26; Matthew 28, 3; Luke 24, 5; John 20, 12; and Acts 1, 10. The expression *vestimenta . . . alba sicut nix* is used of Christ in his transfiguration (Matthew 17, 2; cf. Mark 9, 3).

44. See above, p. 76.

45. "Darbietungsformen der Mystik bei Mechthild von Magdeburg", in *Märchen, Mythos, Dichtung. Festschrift zum 90. Geburtstag Friedrich von der Leyens,* ed. Hugo Kuhn, Kurt Schier (Munich, 1963), pp. 375–399.

46. Not only in the introduction and notes to his edition, but in *Il libro della "Vita Nuova",* 2nd ed. (Florence, 1970).

47. It should be noted that, notwithstanding the traditional insertion of a definite article—"*Das* fliessende Licht der Gottheit"—which is perpetuated even on the title-page of the admirable new edition, Mechthild herself chose the indefinite article—"Dis buoch heisset *ein* vliessendes lieht der gotheit"—and insists that God gave her the title in this precise form: "It shall be called a flowing light *(ein vliessende lieht)* of my godhead" (*Licht,* p. 5, 7 and 10–11).

48. "Darbietungsformen", p. 378.

49. *Licht, Prolog,* pp. 4, 1–5, and 5, 8 *(Ich han es gemachet).*

50. *Licht,* p. 12, printed as prose.

51. *Licht,* p. 19, printed as prose throughout; but I think it preferable here to distinguish the rhymed passage from the unrhymed one.

The citations of Bynum are from her book *Holy Feast and Holy Fast: The Religious Significance of Food to Medieval Women* (Berkeley-Los Angeles-London 1987), pp. 276, 289. Cf. also Bynum's essay "The Body of Christ in the Later Middle Ages", in her recent volume *Fragmentation and Redemption* (New York, 1991), in which she shows that in late medieval art "the wound of Christ and the breast of Mary are clearly parallel in picture after picture" (p. 102, and Figures 3.13–14).

52. *Licht,* pp. 44–45, the whole passage printed as verse.

53. *Licht,* p. 83, printed as prose.

54. *Licht,* pp. 39–40, printed as prose throughout. Again I have thought it preferable to indicate typographically the transition to a heavily rhymed passage.

55. *Licht,* p. 109, printed as prose.

56. *Licht,* pp. 9–10, the whole passage printed as prose.

57. *Women Writers* (cit. n. 1), esp. pp. 217–228.

58. *Mirouer* 52 (pp. 152–154; MS Chantilly, Condé F xiv 26, fol. 40r–v).

59. *Mirouer* and MS have *entree;* but the Latin version, which has "Haec anima, dicit Amor, est *inancorata* intra affluentias divini amoris" (p. 153), shows that the correction to *aencree* is needed.

60. The Latin, "sicut ferrum vestitur igne et suam propriam speciem seu similitudinem perdit", makes clear that *perdue* has *le fer* as its subject.

61. MS has *mue,* wrongly emended in *Mirouer* to *mue<e>:* the object is *le fer.*

62. MS has: *qui est [de s] nee de ses dons.* But here the copyist's deletion may well indicate what was the correct original order.

63. I have arranged these ten lines, printed as prose in *Mirouer,* in poetic form. In the MS, the copyist put bars at the close of what I give as verses 1, 2, 4, and 5, and a full stop at the close of 3, 8, and 10—indicating a certain, even if incomplete, awareness of the symmetries in these lines.

64. *Vita Nuova* III, 10 *(A ciascun'alma presa e gentil core);* XX, 3 *(Amore e 'l cor gentil son una cosa).* Behind Dante's formulation lies the canzone of his "father" in the art of poetry, Guido Guinizelli: *Al cor gentil rempaira sempre amore* (ed. Gianfranco Contini, *Poeti del Duecento,* Milan-Naples, 1960, II, 460–464). Dante returns to the theme once more with the words he gives Francesca in *Inferno* V, 100: *Amor, ch'al cor gentil ratto s'apprende.*

65. With *oultre divine,* compare for instance, in Eriugena's translation of the Dionysian *De divinis nominibus,* chap. 2 (*P.L.* 122, 1121 A): *Unita quidem totius divinitatis sunt . . . superbonum,* superdeum, *superessentiale, supervivens, supersapiens,* where *superdeum* corresponds to τὸ ὑπέρθεον in the Greek (*P.G.* 3, 640 B). Similarly in chap. 13 (1170 D), *superdivinitas* renders ὑπερθεότης (*P.G.* 3, 981 A). Eriugena does not have an expression *superpax,* but in chap. 11, *De pace,* writes of *supermanans magnitudo pacificae generationis* (1166 A; cf. *P.G.* 3, 952 A).

For the iron and fire imagery in Eriugena, compare for instance *Periphyseon,* I, *P.L.* 122, 451 AB (citing Maximus), or V, ibid., 879 B, where "iron or any other metal, molten in fire, is seen to be transmuted into fire, so that it seems to be pure fire, even though the substance of the metal remains preserved. In the same way I think bodily substance will pass into soul . . . and soul similarly will be moved *(movebitur)* into intellect, so that in this it is preserved more beautiful and more like God". For Marguerite, Guarnieri cites a passage from St Bernard, *De diligendo Deo,* X, 28—yet Bernard's text is not as close to her as Eriugena's: the point of the comparison, in which iron becomes "most like to fire", is that "in the saints, all human affection must melt away, and the will must be transfused wholly into God". Yet it is altogether possible that it was a later mystical work using such imagery, rather than the text of Eriugena himself, which stimulated Marguerite's phrasing.

66. Compare also Marguerite's lyrical farewell to the virtues (*Mirouer* 6, p. 24), of which I have given a text in *Women Writers*, p. 275 (discussion ibid., p. 222).

67. Cf. *Licht*, pp. xviii–xix: the manuscripts Rb (mid-fourteenth century) and Ra (early fifteenth century) are the only direct witnesses to the Latin version, *Lux divinitatis*. On the poetic reasons against identifying Dante's Matelda with Mechthild of Magdeburg, cf. my observations in *The Medieval Poet and his World* (Rome, 1984), pp. 396–400.

68. *V.N.* XII, 3–4. On the Boethian reminiscences, see esp. De Robertis' notes *ad loc.*, pp. 72–73.

69. On the background of this image of circle, centre and circumference, see my observations in *Fabula* (cit. chap. II, n. 5), pp. 144–153, and in *Intellectuals and Poets in the Middle Ages* (Rome, 1992), pp. 236–240.

70. "Tradition and the Individual Talent", in his *Selected Prose*, ed. John Hayward (London, 1953), p. 27.

71. *Convivio* II, xii: see especially the fine new edition and commentary by Cesare Vasoli and Domenico De Robertis, in *Dante Alighieri, Opere minori* I, 2 (Milan-Naples, 1988), 201–212.

72. This aspect of the *Vita Nuova,* and the hagiographic background of Dante's individual cult, has been illuminatingly studied by Vittore Branca, "Poetica del rinnovamento e tradizione agiografica nella *Vita Nuova*", *Studi in onore di Italo Siciliano* (Florence, 1966), I, 123–148.

73. *V.N.* III, 3.

Additional note

A copy of Otto Prinz's edition of Aethicus' *Cosmographia* (signalled as forthcoming on p. 120, n. 35, and published in Munich, 1993) reached me in the same days as the proofs of this book. While Prinz brings major scholarly advances—especially as regards text, manuscript transmission, and study of vocabulary—I was happy to note that there is no overlap with my discussion of Aethicus in chap. I above, and that this needs modification only in a couple of minor points. Prinz's long introduction does not touch on the questions of tone and form—the "Menippean elements"—discussed here. As to authorship, I still think it likeliest, for the reasons of style and content adduced above, that the author was an Irishman on the Continent and not a genuine Scythian or Istrian or "Avar of Turkish stock", as Prinz suggests (p. 18). Is it not significant in this regard that his geographical knowledge of Greece and Macedonia is "astonishingly" confused (*sic* Prinz,

p. 16), and that so many of his place-names in Eastern Europe and Asia Minor "defy explanation" (p. 21)—i.e., on my view, are pure inventions? As to the date: according to Prinz, the reference to a lost MS of 754 is erroneous (p. 9); yet since the extant MS L, assigned by Bischoff to Freising in the period before 783, is full of scribal corruptions, and presupposes two antecedent copies (*sic* Prinz, p. 61), I still incline to put the composition of the *Cosmographia* a little earlier than "ca. 750", the date proposed by Prinz.

In the longer passage of Aethicus that I cite above (p. 16) from D'Avezac's text, there are three divergences from the new edition other than orthographic ones. In l. 3, *aquilarum pennas assumunt,* Prinz (using the earliest MSS) prefers *ad summum.* The passage in Isaiah, however (cf. p. 121, n. 41 above), which Prinz does not note—*assument pennas sicut aquilae*—shows that *assumunt* is needed. In l. 12 Prinz reproduces the MSS: *limphaque arma adsumitur.* D'Avezac's emendation, *lymphâque arena,* avoids the need to construe *adsumitur* actively here (unlikely if the normal active form of this verb was used only just before). In the last line I cite, the later MSS used by D'Avezac have normalised *decipula* (Prinz) to *decipulam.* Prinz's valuable *loci paralleli* include a reference to Isaiah 23, 14 for Aethicus' *ululant naves maris,* and to Daniel 7, 10 *(decies millies centena millia)* for his mode of reckoning the "billion" slain in Alexander's battle with the Albanians.

Since returning the page proofs of this volume, I have been informed that *Étoilette* does not feature in the first (1710) edition of Madame de Murat, and hence could have drawn—even if not exclusively—on Sainte-Palaye's version of *Aucassin et Nicolette.*

Index